Ynard

D1476968

A NEW COURSE IN URDU
AND SPOKEN HINDI

for learners in Britain

by

Ralph Russell

PART 1

External Services Division
School of Oriental and African Studies
University of London

Second edition, 1986

Ralph Russell, 1986

ISBN 0 7286 0131 1

 British Library Cataloguing in Publication Data

Russell, Ralph
    A new course in Urdu (and spoken Hindi) for learners in Britain.
    Part 1
    1. Urdu/Hindi language - Grammar
    I. Title II. University of London. *School of Oriental and African Studies*
    491'.43'83421   PK1933

    ISBN 0 7286 0131 1

This is a second edition of the work first published as A New
Course in Hindustani for Learners in Britain, Part 1.

CONTENTS

Foreword

This book is the second edition of a course which I wrote and published in 1980. Most of you who are reading this will not, of course, have seen the first edition; so I need to tell you something of who the course is for and of what it enables you to learn.

This is Part I of a course consisting of four parts, but Part I is complete in itself, and only those who want to go further need study the other parts - of which more in a moment.

I wrote it to try and meet the needs of those adult learners whose contacts with South Asian settlers here in Britain had inspired them with a desire to learn a language in which they could communicate with those of them who know little or no English. Most of these would-be learners have only a limited amount of time to spare and most of them want above all to understand and speak the language rather than learning how to read and write it. I aimed therefore to write a course which would teach them as quickly as possible to say and to understand the things which come within the range of everyday conversation, covering all the essential structures of the language without moving outside that range.

For those who wanted to go further than this I wrote Parts II and III, and, for those who wanted to learn to read and write the Urdu script, Part IV. All I need say of these here is that for those of you who want to learn to read and write at the same time as learning to understand and speak, Part IV has been written in such a way that you can do so, for it teaches you to read and write in the Urdu script the sentences of Part I roughly in the order in which you meet them in Part I. Those who want fuller details of all four parts can get a leaflet which describes them from me (19 Earlsthorpe Road, London, S.E.26, tel.: 01 778 4535) or from the Publications Officer, School of Oriental and African Studies, University of London, Malet Street, London, WC1E 7HP (tel.: 01 637 2388).

In August 1979, I concluded my foreword to the first edition with these words:

Every teacher worth his salt learns all the time from those he is teaching, and I owe a special debt to all the students to whom I have taught this course. Its publication will bring it within the reach of other students and other teachers. Their experience too is bound to suggest areas where there is room for improvement. As always, I shall be very grateful if they will let me know of their criticisms and suggestions.

This new edition is the outcome of that experience. Since the first edition was published in 1980 3,000 copies have been sold and substantial numbers of people have taught and learnt from it. I and/ or others have taught from it in Leeds, Sheffield and Rotherham, Birmingham, Dewsbury and Batley, Huddersfield, Blackburn, Manchester,

Bradford, central London, Waltham Forest, Tower Hamlets, and elsewhere. Also, in widely-scattered areas of Britain students have learnt from it on their own, without the help of a teacher. Thus a lot of experience has accumulated over the past five years.

Those who have learnt from the course have always included a high proportion of professional teachers, and quite a number of them have gone on to teach from it very effectively. They have brought to their learning and teaching many skills and much experience which I myself lacked, including those of teaching English as a second language to Asian adults, and teaching in schools - primary, secondary, and supplementary - and it is above all their experience which has inspired the changes incorporated in this second edition, which has been completely re-written from start to finish. My warmest thanks go to all of them, and especially to Alison Shaw, Ian Russell, Marion Molteno and Sughran Choudhry for all the time, energy and careful thought which they have so willingly given. To which I should add that I alone am responsible for the final shape which I have given to it.

For those who are familiar with the first edition, I should draw attention to the main changes I have made. First, the change of title. The course was originally entitled A New Course in Hindustani, for reasons which will be clear from what you will be told in the Introduction. But, as I should perhaps have foreseen, this sometimes led to misunderstandings of its purpose, and I have therefore changed the title to its present form.

A second change is the omission of those parts of the first edition which were directed mainly at the teacher rather than the student. Alison Shaw is now preparing a separate teacher's guide, and I have therefore left in the course only such matter as the students themselves need. (Teachers should therefore note that they will no longer find in this course any indication of how to teach it. For this they will need now to go to the teachers' guide.) All the same, bearing in mind that there will still be many, as there have been hitherto, who use the book and the accompanying cassettes to study on their own, I have, as before, included detailed step-by-step guidance which would not have been needed for students who are learning with the constant help of a teacher.

Other changes can be left to speak for themselves, but I must express my warmest thanks to the author of one of them, namely to Brian Todd, who drew the pictures which are a new feature in this edition, and which, as learners and teachers in Oxford and London have already seen, make the learning of the materials they illustrate an easier and more enjoyable task.

A course like this will, in a sense, always be a draft, for experience will go on revealing needs for improvement. As before, I hope that criticisms and suggestions will continue to come in, so that further revisions can in due course be made.

It may be helpful to say something about the organisation of courses for learners of Urdu/Hindi. Experience shows that the format which seems to suit the needs of the greatest number of learners is that of a weekend course in which teaching begins on Friday evening and ends on Sunday at tea time, and which may include an optional session on Saturday evening. After an interval of some weeks, a second course on the same pattern is given, and further courses can be given at this sort of interval as long as students want them. They will need at least three or four such courses, at, say, 3-monthly intervals and with regular follow-up study between courses, to assimilate Part I thoroughly.

Better still, where circumstances allow, is a five-day course of the kind pioneered at Lancashire College, Chorley. Here the courses are fully residential, though they can also accommodate students who will attend every day from 9.15 in the morning to 8.30 at night. Here the general pattern is Urdu/Hindi all the way, including in tea and coffee breaks and meal times, and since students each have a study bedroom and are provided with full board they are free to do nothing but study for the greater part of their waking hours. Such courses usually run from Sunday tea-time to Friday tea-time. Similar courses are sometimes run from a Tuesday evening of one week through to Tuesday tea-time of the following week. And a similar course of a fortnight's duration could probably be mounted if there were a viable demand for it.

This is perhaps not the place to go into further detail about courses that can be provided, but those interested can write to me (with s.a.e. please) or phone me, and I will gladly send them details.

Ralph Russell,
October 1985.

Introduction: Urdu, Hindi, 'Hindustani', and the other languages of South Asian settlers

The great majority of Asian settlers in Britain come from an area which before 1947 was called India.   But that area today comprises the three states of Pakistan, India and Bangladesh, and obviously therefore cannot be called by its old name.   The Americans long ago adopted the sensible practice of calling it South Asia and I shall generally do the same.   (I suppose that it is because South Asians form the largest group of immigrants from Asia which our contemporary colour-conscious society identifies as such that they are so frequently called just 'Asians'. But that is not a very logical usage, first because South Asia is only a part of that great continent, and secondly because other Asians from others parts of it (e.g. from Hong Kong) have also settled here in considerable numbers.   Still, the current usage is probably too firmly established now to be changed.)

It is from three relatively small areas of South Asia, each separated from the others by hundreds of miles, that most of the settlers come.   These are Panjab (of which there is both a Pakistani and an Indian part), Gujarat, and Bengal.   (Bengal too has two parts - Indian Bengal and Bangladesh.)   They have as their mother tongues the languages known, correspondingly, as Panjabi, Gujarati, and Bengali.   All three languages are closely related, and all belong to the same great language family as the languages of Europe - which, incidentally, makes them a good deal easier to learn than most British natives suppose.   You will notice at once that Urdu and Hindi do not figure in this short list at all, and you will naturally want to know why in that case you are being invited to learn either or both of them.   The short answer is, Because it is the language that most South Asian settlers expect you to learn, and because it is the one language understood by large numbers of people of all the language communities I have named.   Why this is so needs explaining at some length.

South Asia has always been a part of the world in which people of different regions have spoken different languages - and in which a language which was not the mother-tongue of most of them has been spoken as a second language - what Indians sometimes call a 'link language' - over a far wider area than any one of these regions occupied.   Over the north and centre of the sub-continent, what is now Urdu/Hindi has for several centuries been a language of this kind.   It came into existence, and reached maturity, during the five centuries from about 1200 to 1700 when Muslims from the North-West invaded, settled, and established dynasties which in their heyday dominated all the north and centre of the country.   Their language of administration and culture was Persian, and as always happens in such historical circumstances, a knowledge of the language of the rulers was acquired by large numbers of their subjects, and many words of the language entered the different indigenous languages. (The same thing happened with English when this became the language of the rulers of India.)   This influx of Persian words occurred not only in

the regional languages, but also in the more widely-spread second
language of the great northern plains.   This language was based upon
the dialect of the area comprising Delhi and the belt of territory
which now constitutes the western part of U.P. (Uttar Pradesh).   In
its varying forms (of which more later), and at different periods of
its history, it has been known by various names, including Hindi,
Urdu, and Hindustani.

Up to a certain level of social and inter-regional intercourse,
the language known by these different names is, in its spoken form,
a single language within which only minimal variations occur.   These
mostly relate to the religious differences within the many millions of
people (perhaps 200 million) who speak it.   Thus a Muslim will call some
of the days of the week by names that no Hindu or Sikh will use, because
these days (e.g. Friday, the day of congregational prayer) have some
special significance for him which is expressed in the names by which
he calls them.   But if he wants to ask the price of potatoes or the way
to the post office he will say exactly the same as anyone else will say.

Beyond this level divergencies increase.   Since the language is
not only a 'link language' but also the mother-tongue of millions of
speakers, it has, like the regional languages, a developed literary form,
and at this level two significant differences appear between two forms
known respectively as Hindi and Urdu.   In the first place, the two are
written in completely different scripts - Urdu in a modified form of the
Arabic script and Hindi in a script called Devanagari, or simply Nagari.
And secondly, while Urdu literature is overwhelmingly the work of Muslim
writers, portrays the lives of Muslims, and draws its higher vocabulary
from Persian, Hindi literature is overwhelmingly the work of Hindu
writers, portrays the lives of Hindus, and draws its higher vocabulary
from Sanskrit.

The divergence began to grow rapidly during the period of British
rule.   Amongst the Hindus the feeling grew - whether rightly or wrongly
is something that need not concern us here - that the influence that the
Muslims had exercised on the indigenous Indian languages was an alien
one, and should be greatly diminished, if not eliminated.   This feeling,
inevitably, was stronger among the educated than it was among the
uneducated.   Obviously, and equally inevitably, it was the educated who
wrote the Hindi books and newspapers, employing in them the kind of
language that met the new self-imposed standards; and a literary Hindi
thus came into existence which differs fairly substantially from the
spoken Hindi of the great mass of less highly educated people who have
Hindi as their mother tongue.   Of course, the relation between the
spoken and written versions is not an unchanging one.   Many words which,
though common in the written version, were a generation ago perhaps rarely
used in speaking, have now found acceptance in speech as well, and the
spread of literacy will doubtless take this process further.   But
however that may be, as things stand at present, learners of Hindi have
to come to terms (as learners of Urdu do not) with a situation in which
they must learn words which they may speak but not write, and other
words which they may write but not speak; and the spoken language is

much closer to Urdu than the written language.[1]   Thus there is a language in everyday use that may equally well be called Urdu or Hindi - and indeed _is_ called by both names;   for Muslims will call it Urdu, while non-Muslims will call it Hindi.   It is this common language that has often been called Hindustani, and I adopted this name for it in the first edition of this course.   However, since the great majority of its speakers do not use this name for it, and indeed view its use with some hostility, I have now abandoned it.   Though one cannot find an acceptable name of this language, the reality of its existence and of its usefulness is attested by its employment as the medium of the mass-circulation Indian films, which are seen, enjoyed and understood all over India and in the cinemas in areas of South Asian settlement - Indian and Pakistan alike - in this country.   It is attested also by the fact that this is the language long employed by the BBC in its programmes for South Asian immigrants, though some would feel that the BBC tends towards the Urdu side of centre.   Written in the Urdu script it becomes Urdu;   and written in the Devanagari script it becomes Hindi.[2]

In the language which this course teaches probably something like 90% of the words used can equally well be classified as Urdu and as Hindi;   but here and there it will go beyond the range of a vocabulary which could without any doubt be so classified and where it does I have given the specifically Hindi variants.   I could not have done this on my own, for I do not regard myself as sufficiently competent in Hindi. I am therefore most grateful to my colleague Rupert Snell, Lecturer in Hindi at SOAS, who undertook this task and gave many hours of his time both to consultation with native speakers of Hindi and to sessions with me.

One more thing needs to be said about the language needs you are seeking to meet.   Throughout South Asia a situation exists in which people will, in the home and with their kin and their friends, commonly speak one language, while in a wider social context they will speak another language - and I mean another _language_, not simply a standardised, educated form of their own native speech.   The kind of problems which this may create for the foreign learner can best be illustrated by describing the situation which obtains in the Pakistani community here. Most of them come from the Panjab or from that part of Kashmir which is

---

1.   More precisely, the situation is that very large numbers of Hindi speakers use in speech a language which diverges significantly from standard written Hindi.   The extent of the divergence differs somewhat from region to region and also in many cases according to the standard of education of the speaker.
2.   It may be as well to remark at this point that the absence in Urdu of a gap between the spoken and the literary forms comparable to that which exists in Hindi is not to be explained in terms of an alleged Muslim tolerance and an alleged Hindu bigotry and narrow-mindedness. The Muslims, tolerant and bigoted alike, were, so to speak, stuck with a situation that denied any scope for a purism like that of the Hindi litterateurs;   because Urdu was by definition a mixed language - a language in which an Indian structure sustained the weight of a mass of originally non-Indian words.

effectively part of Pakistan, and their mother tongue is one
variety or another of Panjabi. Most of them are village people.
Most of the women, and quite a number of the men, have never had any
formal education of any kind, and those of them who have, have rarely
acquired much more than an ability to read and write Urdu. Unlike
their fellow-Panjabis, the Indian Sikhs, who take a great pride in
their native Panjabi language and have played the major part in its
development to its present position as one of the major literary
languages of India, they accord a very low status to their own native
speech. Many think that it 'cannot be written' and it is not taught
in the schools, where from the outset Urdu is the medium of instruction.
So strong is this sense of its inferior status that Pakistani Panjabis
do not think it proper to use Panjabi at all except in the home and
in informal conversation with their peers. For all other purposes the
'proper' language is Urdu, the national language of Pakistan. In my
own personal experience an uneducated woman who wants to write to her
brother will get a more literate friend to write a letter in Urdu, and
even when she speaks a message to him on tape will speak Urdu and not
Panjabi, even though, obviously, her Panjabi will be correct and her Urdu
very often faulty. For the same sort of reasons it is Urdu that they
will expect a foreigner to learn if she wants to communicate freely with
those who do not know English. But since their own knowledge of Urdu
is often rather rudimentary, you will quite often find that the Urdu
you are learning, confined though it is to the simple everyday area of
the language, will not always correspond to the Urdu they speak, and you
may on occasion have to use a word other than that which this course
teaches you. For example, the correct Urdu for 'husband' is 'xavynd'
or 'ʃəwhər', but many Pakistani women may not know these words, and even
if they do, will speak of their husband as their 'admi' – which means
simply 'man', or, more accurately, 'human being', since it can, in
correct Urdu, comprehend both sexes. When you find this sort of non-
correspondence, you will have to adapt accordingly, and if the situation
is sometimes an unexpected and momentarily disconcerting one, don't make
the mistake of thinking that it is also a difficult one. It isn't.
This sort of ad hoc adjustment is very easily made.

But almost everything in this course will be understood by most of
those with whom you want to communicate. If in your case it is Pakistani
Panjabis that you come into contact with, you will find that once you have
learnt adequate Urdu, their resistance to the idea of your also learning
Panjabi may well diminish. So if by that time you have acquired an
appetite for it, you can go on to that next!

How to use this book

In this book I try to meet at one and the same time the needs of two different kinds of user. Whichever kind you are, you will need to use both the book and the cassettes that go with it.

Some of you will have begun learning Urdu in a class taught by at least two teachers. If you are one of these, you will have been learning first orally, and will have been told not to look at the book, and not to write anything while this oral teaching/learning is going on. For you, then, this book is for you to recognise, to see recorded in writing, and to learn to write yourself, what you have already learnt over the air, and so to consolidate what you already know. To help you do this, the book will often explain in rather more detail than you were given in class the structure and logic of the sentences you have learnt. As you will already know, the division of the book into units is, generally speaking, made theme-wise. So the units are not all of equal length, and some will take you longer to work through than others.

Others will be working on their own, without teachers. So the book is written in a way that will, I hope, enable them, working at every stage with both book and accompanying cassettes, to do what others have learnt to do in class. If you are this kind of learner I want you as the first stage in every unit to concentrate on listening to the sentences and to be content with getting only the general sense of what they're about; first time round, try to do this without looking at the book. Then listen again, reading them as you do so and noting at the same time both how the sounds are spoken and how they are written down. Even in unit one I think you can do this. You know from its title that it's about names. The first sentence is:

swniye. mera nam Alison həy. [addressing Bashir] kəhiye, ap ka nam kya həy?

and this means

Listen; my name is Alison. [addressing Bashir] Say [i.e. Tell me], what's your name?

You don't know all this as you hear it, any more than those who heard it in class did when they heard it. But they will have guessed enough of it correctly to know what's going on, and you too - even though you don't have the help they have from seeing the speakers and noting their expression and their gestures - will probably be able to get the gist. Anyway, try! If you find yourself at sea, then go on ahead a little to the part of the unit that explains in detail what the words mean and gives an English translation of the sentences. But then, having

understood what they mean, go back and do what you felt unable to
do before.   Try this approach again with each new set of sentences.
Don't go to the <u>full</u> explanations except where you can't do what you're
asked to do first.   This procedure isn't a pointless one.   In real
life (so to speak) outside the class and without the book in your hand
this is exactly the way in which you'll encounter the language, hearing
along with things you recognise things that are new and strange to you,
and you should learn to handle this without anxiety, registering what
you know, guessing intelligently from this the general sense of what
you <u>don't</u> know, and verifying the exact meanings afterwards.   It's in
order to help you get used to this and feel relaxed about it that I
arrange the material in the way I do.

   After each unit you will find one or more yellow pages.   These
set out in question and answer form the key things you have learnt in
the unit.

   You should work in threes to get the best use out of these, and
at least one of the three should be a woman and at least one a man.
Generally the questioner can be either female or male;   it won't
usually matter which.   Only if you have people of both sexes in your
group (which needn't be limited to three members, though there shouldn't
be more than about six), can you practice the variation of gender which
so many of the language forms reflect.   You can practise on the yellow-
page materials even if you have no teacher and/or Urdu/Hindi speaker
with you.   At the least ambitious you can simply read from the book, with
one reading the questions and the others reading the answers as
appropriate.   (Swap from time to time, so each gets practice in both
asking and answering.)   Then you can have one of you operating looking
at the book and checking from it the answers of others given without
looking at the book.   For the benefit of those of you who can enlist
the help of an Urdu or a Hindi speaker I shall prepare two supplements
to this book in which the sentences will be written respectively in Urdu
and Hindi script.   (Most Urdu and Hindi speakers, understandably, can't
read the Roman script fluently, since they've never had any need to learn
it.)   These yellow pages will also help you (and your teacher) check up
quickly and easily what has been covered in which unit.   For the same
reason I have given a very detailed list of contents and also where
necessary provided sub-heads in the units; so you should be able to find
what you want quite easily as and when you want it.

   The list of contents, and the index of words at the end of the
book, serve another purpose too.   If in (e.g.) unit 4 you encounter
something which isn't explained and which you don't understand, that will
mean that (unless I've slipped up) it's been explained already in a
previous unit.   So if you look at the contents and/or index you'll be
able to find out where the explanation is and turn back and refresh your
memory.

   You ought to do that anyway - turn back repeatedly to refresh your
memory.   It's a good idea almost every time you pick up the book to
begin reading from unit 1, even if your current task is to learn (e.g.)
unit 4.   Only when you've found two or three times in succession that
there was nothing in unit 1 which you hadn't already grasped thoroughly
should you begin next time from unit 2.

If you want to get on as quickly as you can, you should <u>speak</u> the language whenever you get the chance.   Do that from the <u>very</u> beginning.   When you've learnt the sentences in unit 1, <u>use</u> them in talking with people, even though you can't yet say more than these sentences.   Most Asians who know Urdu/Hindi will be pleased to see the results of your efforts to learn the language and will be supportive and encouraging.   Make sure that you can speak the sentences correctly and fluently.   All you need to achieve this is practice, and practising speaking them is something you can do on your own, though it's better to meet with one or more of your fellow students - <u>regularly</u> if you're wise! - to do this. I I've already explained how you can use the yellow pages to help you in this way.

And that, I think, is enough for the present by way of guidance. I shall be suggesting other useful ways of making what you learn stick at appropriate points as you work through the book.

As you do so I shall be most grateful if you will note any mistakes you notice and jot down ideas of how the book could be improved.   There may well be mistakes that, in spite of all the checking, have still slipped through, and equally there may well be occasions where you feel you can suggest improved presentation and explanation; because neither I nor anyone else has yet had the opportunity to teach from this second edition and so make the modifications in the material which the actual experience of teaching it nearly always suggests.   So do please write! My address and phone number are given in the Foreword.

Unit 1.   Names

Telling people your name;   asking them theirs;
telling and asking others' names;   'Yes' and 'No'

1.1 My name, your name, his name, her name

Listen to these sentences.   First listen to them without looking
at the book, and see how much you can make out.   (You know that they'll
be about people's names.)   Then listen to them again and read them as
you listen.   Two notes about them: First, I've numbered the sentences.
This is just to make it easier for you to find a particular sentence
easily when I refer you back to it later in the unit.   Secondly, you'll
notice that I've used some letters in a way you're not used to.   For
the present, don't worry about them; I'll be explaining them in a moment.

1.   Alison   swniye.   mera nam Alison[1] həy. [addressing Bashir]
                  kəhiye, ap ka nam kya həy?

2.   B.   mera nam bəʃir həy.

3.   A.   phyr kəhiye; ap ka nam kya həy?

4.   B.   mera nam bəʃir həy.

5.   A.   əwr mera nam kya həy?

6.   B.   ap ka nam Alison həy.

7.   [A - addressing Chris] ap ka nam kya həy?

8.   C.   mera nam Chris həy.

9.   A.   əwr mera nam kya həy?

10.   C.   ap ka nam Alison həy.

11.   A.   Mary, ap kəhiye; mera nam kya həy?

12.   M.   ap ka nam Alison həy.

13.   A.   səb kəhiye, 'ap ka nam Alison həy'.

14.   [All]   ap ka nam Alison həy.

15.   A.   ʈhik həy.   bəhwt əccha!   ʃabaʃ!

---

1.   In this course names in the Urdu/Hindi sentences are underlined.
     I do not use capitals for Asian names.   In neither the Urdu nor the
     Hindi script, which some of you will be learning, are there any letters
     corresponding to our capitals.

16. A.   <u>Sue</u>, yn se puchiye, 'ap ka nam kya həy?'

17. Sue – addressing <u>Niru</u>   ap ka nam kya həy?

18. N.   mera nam <u>niru</u> həy.

19. A.   <u>Tom</u>, ap kysi se puchiye, 'ap ka nam kya həy?'

20. Tom – addressing Som   ap ka nam kya həy?

21. Som   mera nam <u>som</u> həy.

22. A.   <u>bəʃir</u>, yn ka nam kya həy?

23. B.   yn ka nam <u>Terry</u> həy.

24. A.   phyr kəhiye.

25. B.   yn ka nam <u>Terry</u> həy.

26. A.   əwr yn ka nam kya həy?

27. B.   yn ka nam <u>Jane</u> həy.

28. A.   phyr kəhiye.

29. B.   yn ka nam <u>Jane</u> həy.

30. A.   yn ka pura nam kya həy?

31. B.   yn ka pura nam <u>Jane Callaway</u> həy.

1.2 <u>The script, and some sounds. The vowels; y, ʃ, th, c, aspiration</u>

Now notice how these sentences are written.   In this course we
use a script which as far as possible follows the principle of one
sound, one symbol; one symbol one sound.   For example 'w' standing
on its own will always represent the sound which occurs in the very
first word of sentence 1. - s<u>w</u>niye; and whenever you want to
represent this sound in writing you will always write <u>w</u>.   There are
only a few common exceptions to this 'one sound, one symbol' rule, and
the three most common ones are illustrated in the sentences you have
just heard.   (More of this in a moment.)

It's very important that you should learn to read and write this
script accurately right from the outset.   My experience is that learners
who haven't believed me when I said this, have later come to realise that
they <u>ought</u> to have believed me.   So even if at this moment you're not
convinced, take it from me that it <u>is</u> necessary and act accordingly.

It seems sensible here to list and explain the vowels that are used
in Urdu.   Listen to the sentences again, and watch out for them in the
following words:

ə	-	bəʃir, kəhiye]
a	-	ap ka nam] all in sentence 1
y	-	phyr (1), yn (11)
i	-	bəʃir
w	-	swniye (1)
u	-	puchiye (16)
e	-	mera, kəhiye (1)
əy	-	həy
o	-	som (21)
əw	-	əwr (5)

As you see, all the vowel sounds of Urdu/Hindi occur in these sentences.

Now look again at the sentences.   In sentence 1 the first word ends in iye, and the 5th in əy.   And in sentence 5 the first word begins with əw.   These three groupings of letters represent the only common exceptions to the 'one sound, one symbol' rule.

y represents both the short vowel and the consonant sound in, e.g., the final 'ye' of swniye and kəhiye.   In the -iye ending the 'i' is, for reasons you need not bother about for the present, used to represent the sound which elsewhere is represented by 'y', and the 'y' which follows it is the consonant y.

In the other pairs of letters (əy and əw) two letters represent one sound.

In sentence 2, 'ʃ' in 'bəʃir' represents the sound of English 'sh' in 'shall'.

In sentence 3, 'ph' stands for an aspirated 'p'.   (In our script it never represents the 'f' sound).   In Urdu/Hindi very many of the consonants have both an aspirated and an unaspirated version, and some of these present difficulties to English learners.   But with care and practice you can get them right.   This one - ph - isn't difficult for English speakers.

In sentence 15, notice how you pronounce ʈhik.   Urdu/Hindi has two 't's, and neither of them is the same as English 't'.   One is called a dental 't', because you touch the back of your teeth with your tongue to say it.   The word bəhwt, in sentence 15 ends in this dental t. And the other one - this one - is called retroflex 't', because you say it with the tip of your tongue retroflexed, or curled back, and in 'ʈhik', the retroflex 'ʈ' is also aspirated.

Many Urdu/Hindi speakers hear our English 't' as their retroflex, and pronounce it accordingly.   When they take English words into their own language, the 't' nearly always becomes ʈ.

Also in sentence 15, notice how you pronounce əccha. 'c' in our script represents a sound near enough to the 'ch' sound in the English word 'which'.

Two points: first, in əccha the 'c' is doubled. In English, most double consonants aren't pronounced double (or, as some people equally sensibly describe it, 'long'). But you do hear the doubling/ lengthening in such words as 'unnecessary'. In Urdu/Hindi all double letters are pronounced accordingly.

Secondly, the sound is aspirated. If you want to make sure you're aspirating the cch when you say əccha, hold a piece of paper in front of your mouth when you say it. If it moves, you're aspirating. If it doesn't you're not.

In sentence 16 note again that the 'ch' of 'puchiye' is aspirated.

I shall where necessary explain what other letters stand for as and when you first meet them; and an appendix (pp. 216-218) lists all of those that need explaining: so you can refer to that whenever you want to.

Now read the sentences again, and note carefully how each sound is written.

Now, without looking at the written version, listen to them and try to write them down correctly. Then compare what you've written with the text in the book, and make any corrections you need to.

Repeat this exercise until you're no longer making any mistakes.

1.3 Notes on the sentences 1-31, and English translation

If you've been taught these sentences in class you'll have quickly realised from the context and from the teacher's gestures what each of them means. Even if you're working on your own, without a teacher, you will probably have guessed their meanings correctly. Here are the points you need to note.

The word order is different from that of English

>   mera nam Alison həy

means, word for word

>   my name Alison is

>   ap ka nam kya həy?

means

>   your (= ap ka - two words in Urdu - for reasons
>   that need not concern you at this point)
>   name what is?

yn ka (again, two words in Urdu/Hindi) means both
'his' and 'her'.

Here are the sentences again, with a literal translation under
each:

In most cases the translation will itself serve to explain anything
you don't already understand, but I have added notes where necessary.

1. A.   swniye.   mera nam Alison həy.   kəhiye, ap ka nam kya həy?
            Listen.   My name Alison is.   Say, your name what is?

2. B.   mera nam bəʃir həy.
            My name Bashir is.

3. A.   phyr kəhiye;   ap ka nam kya həy?
            Again say, Your name what is?

4. B.   mera nam bəʃir həy.
            My name Bashir is.

5. A.   əwr mera nam kya həy?
            And my name what is?

6. B.   ap ka nam Alison həy.
            Your name Alison is.

7. A.   [addressing Chris] ap ka nam kya həy?
                               Your name what is?

8. C.   mera nam Chris həy.
            My name Chris is.

9. A.   əwr mera nam kya həy?
            And my name what is?

10. C.   ap ka nam Alison həy.
            Your name Alison is.

11. A.   Mary, ap kəhiye;   mera nam kya həy?
            Mary, you say: my name what is?

12. M.   ap ka nam Alison həy.
            Your name Alison is.

13. A.   səb kəhiye, 'ap ka nam Alison həy'.
            All say 'Your name Alison is'.

14. All   ap ka nam Alison həy.
            Your name Alison is.

15. A. ʈhik həy.   bəhwt əccha!   ʃabaʃ!

[That] right is.   Very good!   Well done!

əccha means 'good', but it is a word with many meanings
which depend on context and on the intonation of your
voice.   It can mean 'right' or 'now then', or 'I see';
or it can be used to show that you're moving on to something new.   It can also express surprise:

əccha?
really?

or a sudden realisation of something:

əccha!
Oh, now I see!

16. A. Sue, yn se puchiye, 'ap ka nam kya həy?'

Sue, her from enquire, 'Your name what is?'

Note that in Urdu/Hindi you have no prepositions,
which come 'pre' - i.e. before - the word they refer
to, but postpositions, which come 'post' - i.e. after -
the word they refer to.

17. S. [addressing Niru] ap ka nam kya həy?

Your name what is?

18. N. mera nam niru həy.

My name Niru is.

19. A. Tom, ap kysi se puchiye, 'ap ka nam kya həy?'

Tom, you someone from enquire, 'Your name what is?'

20. T. [addressing Som] ap ka nam kya həy?

Your name what is?

21. S. mera nam som həy.

My name Som is.

22. A. beʃir, yn ka nam kya həy?

Bashir, his name what is?

23. B. yn ka nam Terry həy.

His name Terry is.

24. A. phyr kəhiye.

Again say.

25. B. yn ka nam Terry həy.

His name Terry is.

26. A. əwr yn ka nam kya həy?

And her name what is?

27. B. yn ka nam <u>Jane</u> həy.

Her name Jane is.

28. A. phyr kəhiye.

Again say.

29. B. yn ka nam <u>Jane</u> həy.

Her name Jane is.

30. A. yn ka pura nam kya həy?

Her full name what is?

31. B. yn ka pura nam <u>Jane Callaway</u> həy.

Her full name Jane Callaway is.

1.4 <u>'Yes' and 'No'</u>

Now take the next group of sentences. Follow the same directions as you did with the first group.

32. B. əb swniye. yn ka nam <u>Jane</u> həy? .... <u>Alison</u>, ap bətaiye.

33. A. ji haŋ, yn ka nam <u>Jane</u> həy.

34. B. əwr yn ka nam <u>Terry</u> həy?

35. A. ji haŋ, yn ka nam <u>Terry</u> həy.

36. B. ap ka nam <u>Alison</u> həy?

37. A. ji haŋ, mera nam <u>Alison</u> həy.

38. B. [addressing Jane] əwr ap ka nam? ap ka nam <u>Jane</u> həy?

39. J. ji haŋ, mera nam <u>Jane</u> həy.

40. B. mera nam <u>bəʃir</u> həy?

41. J. ji haŋ, ap ka nam <u>bəʃir</u> həy.

42. B. əb swniye. <u>Alison</u>, bətaiye: [pointing to Chris] yn ka nam <u>Terry</u> həy?

43. A. ji nəhiŋ. yn ka nam <u>Terry</u> nəhiŋ həy. yn ka nam <u>Chris</u> həy.

44. B. phyr kəhiye.

45. A.   ji nəhiŋ.   yn ka nam Terry <u>nəhiŋ</u> hey.   yn ka nam <u>Chris</u> həy.

46. B. [pointing to Jane]   yn ka nam <u>Caroline</u> həy?

47. A.   ji nəhiŋ.   yn ka nam <u>Caroline</u> nəhiŋ həy.   yn ka nam <u>Jane</u> həy.

48. B.   ap ka nam <u>Mary</u> həy?

49. A.   ji nəhiŋ.   mera nam <u>Mary</u> nəhiŋ həy.   mera nam <u>Alison</u> həy.

50. B.   əwr mera nam?   mera nam əkbər həy?

51. A.   ji nəhiŋ.   ap ka nam əkbər nəhiŋ həy.   ap ka nam <u>bəʃir</u> həy.

Do the same exercises on these sentences as you did with sentences 1-31.

I don't think there is any need for me to translate sentences 32-51 in full. A few notes will be enough. (The numbers below refer to the sentences.)

32. əb means 'now'

    <u>bətaiye</u> means 'tell [me]'

Notice that in Urdu/Hindi the order of words in a question is exactly the same as the order of words in a statement. Only the intonation changes.

33. <u>ji haŋ</u> means 'yes'. ŋ after a vowel indicates that the vowel is nasalised.

    <u>ji</u> and <u>haŋ</u> on their own also both mean 'yes', but they sound a bit more offhand and/or abrupt in tone than <u>ji haŋ</u>. So <u>ji haŋ</u> is the form you'd better use.

Many Panjabis reverse the order and say 'haŋ ji', but this isn't standard Urdu/Hindi usage.

43. <u>ji nəhiŋ</u> means 'no'. (Panjabis will often say '<u>nəhiŋ ji</u>', but this isn't standard Urdu usage.)

The <u>nəhiŋ</u> immediately before the verb (<u>həy</u>) means 'not'. In Urdu/Hindi word order, this is where it normally comes - 'His name Terry not is'.

You could shorten some of the replies. For example, the reply to 32 could be

            ji haŋ, <u>Jane</u> həy
            Yes [it]'s Jane   -

notice that you don't need to express the equivalent of 'it' in a separate word. Similarly, the reply to 43 could be

            ji nəhiŋ; yn ka nam <u>Chris</u> həy.

But to repeat the words of the question in full in your answer is not in the least unusual, and you'll rarely hear an Urdu/Hindi speaker replying with a simple <u>ji haŋ</u> or <u>ji nəhiŋ</u>.

You may like to reflect at this point why it is that Asians who learn their English in South Asia, or as adults in England, find difficulty with our 'his' and 'her', and with the change of word order which in English transforms a statement into a question.   Look back at sentences 16, and 22-34, and you will <u>see</u> why.

The next page is a yellow one.   These will recur at intervals throughout the book.   I have already explained how you should use them in <u>How to use this book</u>.

To follow Unit 1

Q = questioner, who may be a woman or a man
W = a woman
M = a man

1. Q.   (to W) ap ka nam kya həy?

2. W.   mera nam .... həy

3. Q.   (to M) əwr ap ka nam kya həy?

4. M.   mera nam .... həy.

5. Q.   (indicating M) yn ka nam kya həy?

6. W/M.   yn ka nam .... həy.

7. Q.   (indicating W) əwr yn ka nam kya həy?

8. W/M.   yn ka nam .... həy.

9. Q.   (indicating W) yn ka pura nam kya həy?

10. W/M.   yn ka pura nam .... həy.

11. Q.   (indicating X) yn ka nam X həy?

12. W/M.   ji haŋ, yn ka nam X həy.

13. Q.   (indicating Y) yn ka nam Z həy?

14. W/M.   ji nəhiŋ, yn ka nam Z nəhiŋ həy;   yn ka nam Y həy.

Unit 2.   What/who/how are you?

2.1 What you are

Listen to these sentences, and get the general sense.   Then
listen to them again, and read them as you listen.   As in unit 1
there'll be some letters which will look strange to you.   I'll
explain them later in the unit.

1. Alison   swniye: məyŋ ʈicər huŋ. bəʃir, ap kya həyŋ?

2. Bashir   məyŋ berozgar[1] huŋ.

3. A.   əwr nəsim, ap kya həyŋ?

4. N.   məyŋ soʃəl vərkər huŋ.

5. A.   əwr [pointing to Terry] yyh[2] kya həyŋ,   ap ko malum həy?

6. N.   ji nəhiŋ, mwjhe malum nəhiŋ.

7. A.   puchiye!

8. N.   Terry, bətaiye, ap kya həyŋ?

9. T.   məyŋ pwlisməyn huŋ.

10. N.   yyh[2] pwlisməyn həyŋ.

11. A.   əwr yyh?[2] [pointing to Lynn]

12. N.   yyh[2] helth vyzyʈər həyŋ.

13. A.   səb kəhiye, 'yyh[2] helth vyzyʈər həyŋ'.

             [All do so]

14. A.   əb səb əwrəteŋ[3] kəhiye.

             [All the women do so]

15. A.   əb səb mərd[4] kəhiye.

             [All the men do so]

16. A.   [to Nasim, pointing to Joan] əwr yyh?[2] yyh[2] bhi helth
             vyzyʈər həyŋ?   ap ko malum həy?

17. N.   ji haŋ, mwjhe malum həy.   yyh[2] helth vyzyʈər nəhiŋ
             həyŋ, yyh[2] nərs həyŋ.

---

1. Hindi (hereafter H.) bekar, which is also quite commonly used in Urdu.
2. H. ye.
3. H. or, striyəŋ.
4. H. admi.

18. A. <u>Betty</u> helth vyzyʈər həyŋ?

19. N. ji nəhiŋ, <u>Betty</u> bhi helth vyzyʈər nəhiŋ həyŋ.
        <u>Betty</u> ɖakʈər həyŋ.

20. A. əwr ap? ap kya həyŋ?

21. N. məyŋ ʈicər huŋ.

22. A. əccha? ap bhi ʈicər həyŋ? məyŋ əwr ap donoŋ
        ʈicər həyŋ.

23. N. ji haŋ.

24. A. əwr <u>Betty</u> ʈicər nəhiŋ həyŋ? ap ko yad həy?

25. N. ji nəhiŋ, mwjhe yad nəhiŋ.

26. A. puchiye.

27. N. [to Betty] ap ʈicər nəhiŋ həyŋ?

28. B. ji nəhiŋ, məyŋ ʈicər nəhiŋ huŋ, məyŋ ɖakʈər huŋ.

29. N. <u>Betty</u> ʈicər nəhiŋ həyŋ. <u>Betty</u> ɖakʈər həyŋ.

30. A. məyŋ əwr <u>nəsim</u> donoŋ ʈicər həyŋ. həm donoŋ ʈicər
        həyŋ. məyŋ, əwr <u>nəsim</u>, əwr <u>som</u> əwr <u>niru</u> səb ʈicər
        həyŋ.

<u>Notes on sentences 1-30</u>

Now notice how the sentences are written. I shall now explain
the new sounds that occur in them. I shall also explain the meanings
of new words.

1. <u>ʈicər</u> is of course the English word 'teacher', adapted to the
Urdu/Hindi sound system - and adapted so thoroughly that <u>none</u> of its
sounds are <u>exactly</u> like those of its English original. Urdu/Hindi
speakers hear our 't' as being more like a retroflex than a dental (see pp.
13-14 above), and when they take an English word into Urdu/Hindi (as
they often do) will pronounce it accordingly. In fact most of them
who learnt their English in South Asia or as adults in Britain speak
English words with this pronunciation when they are speaking English -
just as most English people tend to use <u>their</u> pronunciation for other
languages too. Urdu/Hindi speakers have far more excuse than we do
for using the sounds of their own language when speaking other languages.
Those of them who have learnt English in their own country have very
rarely had the opportunity to learn it from mother-tongue speakers of
English: they have learnt it from teachers who pronounce it as <u>they</u> do.

While we're on this, let me say that listening carefully to the way in which these South Asian speakers of English pronounce it can be very useful to you, because it will help you to see how they adapt English to the sound systems of their own language (all of which bear a close resemblance to that of Urdu/Hindi), and listening to them will help you to see how the characteristic sounds of Urdu/Hindi differ from the English ones you are used to.

ṭ - you met the aspirated retroflex in ṭhik - unit 1, no.15. ṭ is the same sound unaspirated.

r - Urdu/Hindi speakers, like Scottish speakers of English, pronounce the 'r' wherever it comes in an English word.

huŋ - note the nasality - means 'am'.

ŋ - 'n-with-a-tail-on' - shows that the vowel preceding it is nasalised.

4.   v is a sound something between the English v and the English w. Put your upper teeth lightly on your lower lip and try to say an English w and you'll get it right.

British jobs such as these are commonly described by their English names adapted to Urdu/Hindi sounds.

5.   yyh is pronounced in Urdu rather as if it were written yeh.   In Hindi, in these sentences, it would be pronounced and written ye.

5. and 7.   yyh can mean either 'he' or 'she' - just as yn ka can mean either 'his' or 'her'.

In English if you say of someone present 'what is she?' the 'she' in question is likely to be put out, because she will expect you to use her name.   But in Urdu/Hindi yyh[1] is quite alright.

yyh[1] really means 'this' or 'these', and is used for 'she', 'he' or 'they' when the people you are speaking of are present or nearby. For people who are not present you use vwh[2] (pronounced something like 'voh'), which really means 'that' or 'those'.   You can't generally use vwh[1] for people present.

ap ko malum həy? - You to (i.e. to you) known is?   The most usual way of asking if you know something.

6.   mwjhe - to me.   Your pronunciation must let people hear the aspiration.   Note that the sentence means literally, To me not known - i.e. To me [it is] not known.   After nəhiŋ, the Urdu/Hindi equivalents of 'am', 'is', and 'are' can be omitted.

13.   th - an aspirated dental (see p.13 above) - the nearest Urdu/Hindi can get to the English 'th' sound.

---

1.   H. ye.
2.   H. ve.

14. əwrəteŋ[1] - women.

15. mərd[2] - men, males.   Note the dental d̲.

16. bhi - also.

    Note the pronunciation.   It is one syllable, not two.   And it's important to hear the 'h' of bhi.   The easiest way is to say

        hi, hi, hi, hi, hi, ...

and then to slip in the 'b' before it -

        hi, hi, hi, hi, bhi, bhi, ...

Also note about bhi that it always follows immediately after the word to which it applies.   In English you can say

        I'm going to London too

- and according to context, you can mean that you're going to London as well as to somewhere else, or that you, as well as someone else, are going to London.   In Urdu/Hindi you can't be so ambiguous.   You must put bhi immediately after the word it applies to.   So

                    məyŋ bhi t̲icər huŋ
        means
                    I too am a teacher
        while
                    məyŋ t̲icər bhi huŋ

can only mean: I am a teacher too (in the sense of 'I'm not only (e.g.) a singer, but also a teacher'.)

19. d̲akt̲ər - retroflex d̲, retroflex t̲.

22. əccha?   Really? (- but not in a tone that expresses any scepticism!)   Note that in standard Urdu/Hindi you say the equivalent not of 'you and I' but of 'I and you'.

    donoŋ - both.   Dental d̲, nasalised last syllable.

24. ap ko yad həy? - 'you to remembered is?' - i.e. Do you remember?

28. ji nəhiŋ - some speakers might say ji haŋ, in the sense of 'yes, that's right'.

30. həyŋ - Notice that in this sentence həyŋ means 'are'.   Hitherto you have had it in the sense of 'is'.   But həyŋ really is a plural form, while həy is singular.   (In Urdu/Hindi nasality frequently distinguishes plurals from singular, as you will often be seeing from now on.)

    həm means 'we'.

---

1.   H. or, striyəŋ.
2.   H. admi.

The explanation of heyŋ in the sense of 'is' is that in Urdu/Hindi if you are speaking to, or about, someone of equal, superior, or senior status to yourself you use plural verb forms. You will learn more about this in later units.

Now read the sentences carefully again, noting how the sounds are written. Then, without looking at the written version, listen to them on cassette and try to write them down correctly. Then compare what you've written with the text in the book, and make any corrections you need to. Repeat this exercise until you're no longer making any mistakes.

2.2 Who you are

Now take these sentences, and follow the same procedure as before.

31. N.   swniye: məyŋ nəsim huŋ.   yyh[1] Joan həyŋ, əwr yyh[1] Terry
         həyŋ. [pointing to Som] yyh[1] kəwn həyŋ?   Lynn, ap
         bətaiye.   ap ko yad həy?

32. L.   ji nəhiŋ, mwjhe yad nəhiŋ.

33. N.   əccha? ap ko yad nəhiŋ? [Indicating Niru] yn se
         puchiye - nəhiŋ, mwjh se puchiye.

34. L.   yyh[1] kəwn həyŋ?

35. N.   yyh[1] som həyŋ.

36. L.   əccha, yyh[1] som həyŋ.

37. N.   ji haŋ. yyh[1] som həyŋ. əwr yyh?[1] [Pointing to Joan]
         yyh[1] kəwn həyŋ? Betty, ap bətaiye.

38. B.   yyh[1] Joan həyŋ.

39. N.   əwr yyh[1] səb kəwn həyŋ? Alison, ap bətaiye.

40. A.   yyh[1] həyŋ bəʃir, əwr fərida, əwr kəniz.

41. N.   ʈhik həy. ʃabaʃ!

Notes on sentences 31-41

31. kəwn means 'who?'. Make sure you don't aspirate the 'k'.
English speakers often do. If you want to make sure you're not
aspirating it, hold a piece of paper in front of your mouth as you
say it. If the paper moves, you're aspirating it! Practice until
the paper doesn't move.

----

1.   H. ye.

33. əccha? - 'really?'

nəhiŋ, rather than ji nəhiŋ, indicates a sort of urgency.

mwjh se - 'me from' - i.e. from me.   Watch the aspiration!

36. əccha - something like 'I see', but less strong.   It really just indicates that the speaker has registered what she's just been told.

39. həyŋ - here again a real plural - not a courteous plural in the singular sense.

41. yyh həyŋ - the həyŋ could follow the list of names, but where a list is coming the verb commonly precedes it.

Now I'm going to give you fairly natural translations of sentences 1-41.   See if, without looking back at it, you can reconstruct the original,   and then compare and see how far you've managed it.   Minor differences won't necessarily be wrong, but at this stage it's best to stick by the versions the book gives you.

You'll find this re-translation a useful exercise to do repeatedly as you go through the book.   You'll learn more from it than you realise!

1.   A.   Listen: I'm a teacher.   Bashir, what are you?

2.   B.   I'm unemployed.

3.   A.   And Nasim?   What are you?

4.   N.   I'm a social worker.

5.   A.   And (pointing to Terry) what's he?   Do you know?

6.   N.   No, I don't know.

7.   A.   Ask [him]!

8.   N.   Terry, tell [me], what are you?

9.   T.   I'm a policeman.

10.   N.   He's a policeman.

11.   A.   And she? (pointing to Lynn)

12.   N.   She's a health visitor.

13.   A.   All [of you] say [it]: She's a health visitor.

      [All do]

14. A. Now all the women say it.

    [All the women do]

15. A. Now all the men say it.

    [All the men do]

16. A. (to Nasim, pointing to Joan) And she? Is she a health visitor too? Do you know?

17. N. Yes, I know. She's not a health visitor; she's a nurse.

18. A. Is Betty a health visitor?

19. N. No, Betty's not a health visitor either. [Say 'Betty too is not...']. Betty's a doctor.

20. A. And you? What are you?

21. N. I'm a teacher.

22. A. Yes? You're a teacher too? You and I are both teachers.

23. N. Yes.

24. A. And is Betty <u>not</u> a teacher? Do you remember?

25. N. No, I don't remember.

26. A. Ask [her].

27. N. (to Betty) Aren't you a teacher?

28. B. No, I'm not a teacher. I'm a doctor.

29. N. Betty's not a teacher. Betty's a doctor.

30. A. Nasim and I are both teachers. We're both teachers. Nasim, and Som, and Niru, and I are all teachers.

31. N. Listen. I'm Nasim. She's Joan, and he's Terry. (Pointing to Som) Who's he? Lynn, you tell [us]. Do you remember?

32. L. No, I don't remember.

33. N. Really? You don't remember? (Indicating Niru) Ask her. No, ask me.

34. L. Who is he?

35. N. He's Som.

36. L. I see, he's Som.

37. N.   Yes, he's Som.   And she? (pointing to Joan).   Who's she?   Betty, you tell [us].

38. B.   She's Joan.

39. N.   And who are all these?   Alison, you tell [us].

40. A.   They're Bashir, and Farida, and Kaniz.

41. N.   That's right.   Well done!

2.3 How you are

Now listen to these sentences, and follow the same procedure as before.   I'll tell you beforehand that kəyse?/kəysi? means 'how', hal means 'condition', and ʃwkriya means 'thank you'.

42.   Alison [to Niru]   ap kəysi həyŋ?

43.   N.   ʃwkriya,[1] məyŋ ʈhik huŋ.əwr ap?   ap ka kya hal həy?

44.   A.   ʃwkriya,[1] məyŋ bhi ʈhik huŋ.   bəʃir, ap kəyse həyŋ?

45.   B.   ʃwkriya,[1] məyŋ bhi ʈhik huŋ.

ap ka kya hal həy? - 'your what condition is?' - i.e. How are you? Rather more common than ap kəysi/-e həyŋ? (-i in addressing a woman, -e in addressing a man).

Note that in this question the kya precedes the hal.   You can use this word order in asking names too.

ap ka kya nam həy?

Greetings follow different patterns, and mostly vary according to whether those greeting or being greeted are Muslim, Hindu, or Sikh. All this is explained in appendix 2.

To the extent that you still find it useful, repeat the exercise I set you on sentences 1-30.   I shan't from now on be setting this exercise, but you should go on doing it until such time as you have really mastered the script, and should certainly practice it on any sentences in which new symbols occur.

---

1.   H. or, rather more formally, dhənyəvad.

To follow unit 2

1. Q. məyŋ ʈicəɾ huŋ. ap kya həyŋ?

2. W/M. məyŋ .... huŋ.

3. Q. yyh kya həyŋ?

4. W/M. yyh .... həyŋ.

5. Q. kya ap ʈicər həyŋ?

6. W/M. ji haŋ, məyŋ ʈicər huŋ

        or

    ji nəhiŋ, məyŋ ʈicər nəhiŋ huŋ. məyŋ .... huŋ.

7. Q. yyh kəwn həyŋ?

8. W/M. yyh [name] həyŋ.

9. Q. (addressing W) ap ka kya hal həy?

10. W. ʃwkriya,[1] məyŋ ʈhik huŋ.

11. Q. (addressing M) əwr ap? ap ka kya hal həy?

12. M. ʃwkriya,[1] məyŋ bhi ʈhik huŋ.

---

1. H. or, rather more formally, dhənyəvad.

Unit 3.   Where you live

3.1 Listen to these sentences, and get the general sense.   In the first, the speaker is telling the class where she lives and asking Bashir where he lives.   This should give you the clue to the rest. Then listen again, reading the text as you do so.

1. A.   məyŋ Oxford meŋ rəhti huŋ.   bəʃir, ap kəhaŋ rəhte həyŋ?

2. B.   məyŋ bhi Oxford meŋ rəhta huŋ.

3. A.   [to Niru] əwr ap?   ap kəhaŋ rəhti həyŋ?

4. N.   məyŋ bhi Oxford meŋ rəhti huŋ.

5. A.   əwr yyh?[1] [indicating John] yyh[1] kəhaŋ rəhte həyŋ? Joan, ap bətaiye.

6. J.   yyh[1] Reading meŋ rəhte həyŋ.

7. A.   əwr yyh?[1] [indicating Jill] yyh[1] kəhaŋ rəhti həyŋ? John, ap bətaiye.

8. J.   yyh[1] Burton meŋ rəhti həyŋ.

9. A.   əwr Ralph?   Ralph kəhaŋ rəhte həyŋ?   Sue, ap bətaiye.

10. S.   Ralph ləndən meŋ rəhte həyŋ.

11. A.   əwr Marion kəhaŋ rəhti həyŋ?   Som, ap bətaiye.

12. S.   Marion bhi ləndən meŋ rəhti həyŋ.

Notes on these sentences

rəhti huŋ, rəhta huŋ, rəhti həyŋ, rəhte həyŋ

A woman speaking of herself, or anyone speaking to or about a woman (or women) uses the rəhti form.

A man speaking of himself uses the rəhta form.

Anyone speaking to or about a man (or men) uses the rəhte form.

---

1. H. ye.

 əh is pronounced rather like eh.

The t of the -ti, -ta, -te endings is a dental.

meŋ - 'in'.   Another postposition.   You have already met se and ko

> yn se puchiye
> him/her from enquire - i.e. Ask him/her
>
> ap ko malum həy?
> You to known is?   - i.e. Do you know?
>
> Oxford meŋ
> Oxford in   - i.e. in Oxford

Note the word order - subject first, verb last, and the rest in between.   In a question, the question word (in this case kəhaŋ? meaning 'where?') comes just before the verb.

ləndən

Many South Asians pronounce London 'ləndən' with a dental 'd'. I told you on pp.13-14 that when Urdu/Hindi speakers borrow an English word they usually turn English 't' into a retroflex 'ṭ'.   So also with 'd'.   But 'ləndən' is an exception.   South Asians have known the word well for years and for some reason in the earliest borrowings it was the dental, and not the retroflex, which they used for our 't' and 'd'.   Nowadays the use of the retroflex for English 't' and 'd' is practically invariable.

You may as well also note here that towns that South Asians have heard of only after coming to England are likely to be pronounced, near enough, the English way, and there is no harm if you pronounce them in the English way.   (And, of course, those who have learnt their English here will generally pronounce it in the same way as those from whom they have learnt it.)

Notice two things about these sentences.   First, Urdu/Hindi, unlike English, has no separate forms for 'he' and 'she'.   yyh can mean either.   (In these sentences the form of the verb tells you which is meant - unlike English, where the form of the verb is the same regardless of whether the subject is male or female.)   That is why very many South Asians, even those who speak English well, have trouble with our English 'he' and 'she' and are quite likely to use 'he' for both.   You've already seen in Unit 1 that, similarly, yn ka means both 'his' and 'her'.

Secondly, notice that the verb forms used with 'you' and 'he/ she' - ap and yyh[1] - are both plural forms.   (This too, you've already met.)   We don't usually notice it, but English 'you' is also really a plural form.   (We don't say 'you lives'.   We say 'You live'.)   In Urdu the plural is regularly used for courtesy, and not only in the second person ('you') but in the third person ('she, he') as well.   If

---

1.   H. ye.

you translated 'he lives' by the singular form that would imply that you considered the 'he' in question to be of inferior status to yourself. (We shall be saying more of this later on.) And just as I would say <u>yyh</u>[1] kəhaŋ rəhte həyŋ? I would also say

<u>Ken</u> kəhaŋ rəhte həyŋ?

and   <u>Jill</u> kəhaŋ rəhti həyŋ?

<u>English translation of sentences 1-12</u> - for you to re-translate into Urdu.

1. A.   I (f.) live in Oxford.   Bashir, where do you live?

2. B.   I (m.) too live in Oxford.

3. A.   [to Niru] And you?   Where do you (f.) live?

4. N.   I too live in Oxford.

5. A.   And he? [indicating John] Where does he live?   Joan, you tell [us].

6. J.   He lives in Reading

7. A.   And she? [indicating Jill] Where does she live?   John, you tell [us].

8. J.   She lives in Burton.

9. A.   And Ralph?   Where does Ralph live?   Sue, you tell [us].

10. S.   Ralph lives in London.

11. A.   And where does Marion live?   Som, you tell [us].

12. S.   Marion too lives in London.

3.2 Now listen to these sentences: *

13. A.   <u>Jill</u>, ap <u>ləndən</u> meŋ rəhti həyŋ?

14. J.   ji nəhiŋ, məyŋ <u>ləndən</u> meŋ nəhiŋ rəhti huŋ.   məyŋ <u>Burton</u> meŋ rəhti huŋ.

---

*   From this point onwards I shall assume that you will understand that this instruction is shorthand for 1) listen for general sense, without looking at the text, and then 2) listen and read as you do so.

15.. A. <u>niru</u>, ap <u>ləndən</u> meŋ rəhti həyŋ?

16. N. ji nəhiŋ, məyŋ <u>ləndən</u> meŋ nəhiŋ rəhti. məyŋ <u>Oxford</u> meŋ rəhti huŋ.

17. A. <u>bəʃir</u>, ap <u>Reading</u> meŋ rəhte həyŋ?

18. B. ji nəhiŋ, məyŋ <u>Reading</u> meŋ nəhiŋ rəhta huŋ, məyŋ <u>Oxford</u> meŋ rəhta huŋ.

19. A. <u>John</u>, ap <u>Oxford</u> meŋ rəhte həyŋ?

20. J. ji nəhiŋ, məyŋ <u>Oxford</u> meŋ nəhiŋ rəhta, məyŋ <u>Reading</u> meŋ rəhta huŋ.

Notice that Jill replies ....<u>nəhiŋ rəhti huŋ</u>

Niru replies ....<u>nəhiŋ rəhti</u>

Bashir replies ....<u>nəhiŋ rəhta huŋ</u>

and John replies ....<u>nəhiŋ rəhta</u>

Both forms are correct. After <u>nəhiŋ</u> you can miss out <u>huŋ</u> (and also <u>həy</u> and <u>həyŋ</u>) if you want to.

But now notice this sentence:

yyh[1] - <u>Ann</u> - <u>ləndən</u> meŋ nəhiŋ rəht<u>iŋ</u>

Here, because the <u>həyŋ</u> is omitted, the plural form has to be shown by changing <u>rəhti</u> to <u>rəhtiŋ</u>.

3.3 About plurals

I said above that ....<u>rəhte həyŋ</u>, ...<u>rəhti həyŋ</u> in the Urdu/Hindi versions of

He lives....

She lives....

are really plural forms, and explained why these are used. In the sentences that follow - listen to them, reading as you do so - they are <u>real</u> plurals - i.e. plural in meaning as well as in form:

21. Q. yyh[1] - <u>Mark</u> əwr <u>Som</u> - kəhaŋ rəhte həyŋ?

22. A. yyh[1] <u>Oxford</u> meŋ rəhte həyŋ.

---

1. H. ye.

23.   Q.   yyh[1] - <u>Ann</u> əwr <u>June</u> - kəhaŋ rəhti həyŋ?

24.   A.   yyh[1] <u>Cowley</u> meŋ rəhti həyŋ.

25.   Q.   yyh[1] - <u>John</u> əwr <u>Ann</u> - kəhaŋ rəhte həyŋ?

26.   A.   yyh[1] <u>Reading</u> meŋ rəhte həyŋ.

27.   Q.   <u>Alison</u>, ap əwr <u>Mark</u> kəhaŋ rəhte həyŋ?

28.   A.   məyŋ əwr <u>Mark</u> <u>Oxford</u> meŋ rəhte həyŋ.   həm <u>Oxford</u> meŋ rəhte həyŋ.

29.   Q.   <u>June</u>, ap əwr <u>Ann</u> kəhaŋ rəhti həyŋ?

30.   J.   həm <u>Oxford</u> meŋ rəhte[2] həyŋ.

31.   Q.   <u>Sue</u>, ap əwr <u>Judy</u> kəhaŋ rəhti həyŋ?

32.   S.   həm <u>Oxford</u> meŋ rəhti həyŋ.

Notes

25-28.   Where the subjects are mixed male and female the verb takes the masculine form.

30, 32.   In both sentences the speaker is speaking of herself and another woman.   In the first you have <u>rəhte həyŋ</u> and in the second <u>rəhti həyŋ</u>.   The second is, of course, what you'd expect, and in Hindi it is the only correct form.   Panjabi speakers of Urdu also commonly use it, so this is what you will hear for most of the time. However, for some unknown reason, people who have Urdu as their mother tongue <u>always</u> use the -<u>e</u> form with <u>həm</u> (or the equivalent of <u>həm</u> - e.g. <u>məyŋ (f.)</u> əwr Sue....).

---

1.   H. ye.
2.   H. rəhti - and see note below on this sentence.

English translation of sentences 13-32, for you to re-translate into Urdu.

13. A.   Jill, do you live in London?

14. J.   No, I don't live in London. I live in Burton.

15. A.   Niru, do you live in London?

16. N.   No, I don't live in London. I live in Oxford.

17. A.   Bashir, do you live in Reading?

18. B.   No, I don't live in Reading.   I live in Oxford.

19. A.   John, do you live in Oxford?

20. J.   No, I don't live in Oxford, I live in Reading.

21. Q.   Where do they - Mark and Som - live?

22. A.   They live in Oxford.

23. Q.   Where do they - Anne and June - live?

24. A.   They live in Cowley.

25. Q.   Where do they - John and Ann - live?

26. A.   They live in Reading.

27. Q.   Alison, where do you and Mark live?

28. A.   Mark and I live in Oxford - we live in Oxford.

29. Q.   June, where do you and Ann live?

30. J.   We live in Oxford.

31. Q.   Sue, where do you and Judy live?

32. A.   We live in Oxford.

Present tense forms

Feminine forms	Masculine forms

məyŋ rəhti huŋ   məyŋ rəhta huŋ

    I live   I live

həm rəhte həyŋ[1] / rəhti həyŋ[2]   həm rəhte həyŋ*

                                          we live

ap rəhti həyŋ   ap rəhte həyŋ

    you live   you live

yyh[3] rəhti həyŋ   yyh[3] rəhte həyŋ

    She lives   He lives

    They live   They live

* The masculine plural endings also cover mixed masculine and feminine subjects.

---

1. standard Urdu.
2. standard Hindi, and common in Panjabi speakers' Urdu.
3. H. ye.

To follow unit 3

1. Q.   (to W) ap kəhaŋ rəhti həyŋ?

2. W.   məyŋ .... məŋ rəhti huŋ.

3. Q.   (to M) əwr ap?   ap kəhaŋ rəhte həyŋ?

4. M.   məyŋ .... meŋ rəhta huŋ.

5. Q.   (indicating W) yyh[1] kəhaŋ rəhti həyŋ?

6. W/M. yyh[1] .... meŋ rəhti həyŋ.

7. Q.   (indicating M) əwr yyh?[1]   yyh[1] kəhaŋ rəhte həyŋ?

8. W/M. yyh .... meŋ rəhte həyŋ.

9. Q.   (indicating W) yyh[1] .... meŋ rəhti həyŋ?

10. W/M. ji haŋ, yyh[1] .... meŋ rəhti həyŋ

                 or

    ji nəhiŋ, yyh[1] .... meŋ nəhiŋ rəhti həyŋ, yyh[1] .... meŋ rəhti həyŋ.

11. Q.   (indicating M) əwr yyh?[1] yyh[1] .... meŋ rəhte həyŋ?

12. W/M. ji haŋ, yyh[1] .... meŋ rəhte həyŋ

                 or

    ji nəhiŋ, yyh[1] .... meŋ nəhiŋ rəhte həyŋ.   yyh[1] .... meŋ rəhte həyŋ.

13. Q.   (to W) ap Oxford meŋ rəhti həyŋ?

14. W.   ji haŋ, məyŋ Oxford meŋ rəhti huŋ

                    or

    ji nəhiŋ, məyŋ Oxford meŋ nəhiŋ rəhti huŋ, məyŋ .... meŋ rəhti huŋ.

15. Q.   (to M) ap ləndən meŋ rəhte həyŋ?

16. M.   ji haŋ, məyŋ ləndən meŋ rəhta huŋ

                    or

    ji nəhiŋ, məyŋ ləndən meŋ nəhiŋ rəhta huŋ; məyŋ .... meŋ rəhta huŋ.

---

1.   H. ye.

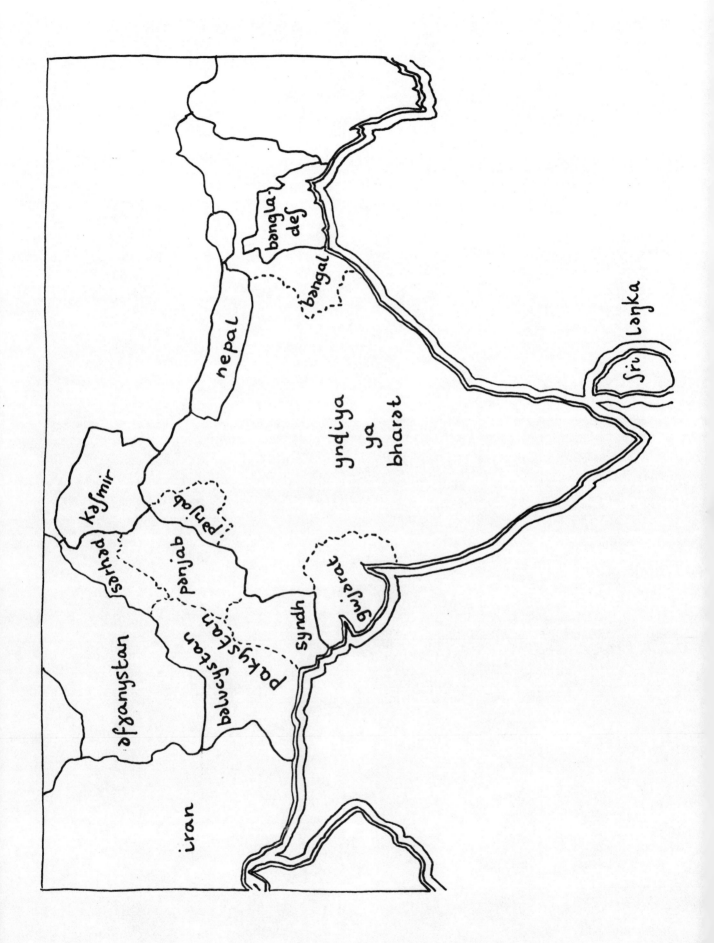

Unit 4.   Countries, places, distances

4.1 South Asia

Look at the map on the page facing this one and listen to these sentences about it, reading them as you do so.   You'll understand everything except a few new words, and these too you'll easily guess by looking at the map as you do so.

1.   yyh jənubi[1] eʃiya həy.

2.   jənubi[1] eʃiya meŋ tin mwlk[2] həyŋ - pakystan, yndiya (ya bharət), əwr bəngladeʃ.

3.   pakystan ke car sube həyŋ - nəmbər ek: sərhəd, nəmbər do: pənjab, nəmbər tin: syndh, nəmbər car: bəlucystan.

4.   bharət ki tera bəɽi bəɽi riyasəteŋ[3] həyŋ.   wn meŋ se tin pənjab, gwjərat, əwr bəngal həyŋ.

5.   pənjabi mwsəlman pakystan meŋ rəhte həyŋ.

6.   pənjabi sykh əwr hyndu bharət meŋ rəhte həyŋ.

7.   bəngali hyndu (əwr kwch mwsəlman) bharət meŋ rəhte həyŋ.

8.   bəngali mwsəlman (əwr kwch hyndu) bəngaldeʃ meŋ rəhte həyŋ.

9.   pakystani pənjabi, sykh pənjabi, gwjərati hyndu, gwjərati mwsəlman, əwr bəngladeʃi mwsəlman - səb kafi tadad[4] meŋ yngləynd men rəhte həyŋ.

Notes on these sentences

1.   jənubi[1] - south, southern.

2.   tin - three

  mwlk[2] - countries

  ya - or

  bharət - note the aspirated 'b'.   Some speakers say hyndostan or hyndwstan (never hyndustan).

---

1.   H. dəkʃyni.
2.   H. deʃ.
3.   H. bəɽe bəɽe prədes.
4.   H. sənkhya.

3. -ke - of

    car - four

    sube - provinces

    nəmbər - number

    ek, do, tin, car - 1, 2, 3, 4

    sərhəd - frontier

    syndh - note the aspirated dental.

4. -ki - of

    -ka, -ki and -ke all mean 'of'. I shall explain later when you use which.

    tera - 13

    bəri bəri - 'big big' - i.e. major, main, most important.

    riyasəteŋ[1] - states

    wn meŋ se - 'them in from', i.e. 'from in them', out of them, of them.

    The sentence means 'India of 13 big big states are' - i.e. India has 13 most important states (India has 'states' and Pakistan has 'provinces').

5. mwsəlman - the usual word for 'a Muslim'. The plural is the same.

ek mwsəlman	one Muslim
car mwsəlman	four Muslims

7. kwch - some

9. kafi - 'enough', quite large

    tadad[2] - number(s)

    kafi tadad meŋ - in quite large numbers

---

1. H. bəṛe bəṛe prədes.
2. H. sənkhya.

Translation of sentences 1-9

1. This is South Asia.

2. In South Asia [there] are three countries - Pakistan, India, and Bangladesh.

3. Pakistan has four provinces - no.1, the Frontier, no.2, Panjab, no.3, Sind, no.4, Baluchistan.

4. India has thirteen major states.   Three of these are Panjab, Gujarat, and Bengal.

5. Panjabi Muslims live in Pakistan.

6. Panjabi Sikhs and Hindus live in India.

7. Bengali Hindus (and some Muslims) live in India.

8. Bengali Muslims (and some Hindus) live in Bangladesh.

9. Pakistani Panjabis, Sikh Panjabis, Gujarati Hindus, Gujarati Muslims, and Bangladeshi Muslims - all in quite large numbers live in Britain.

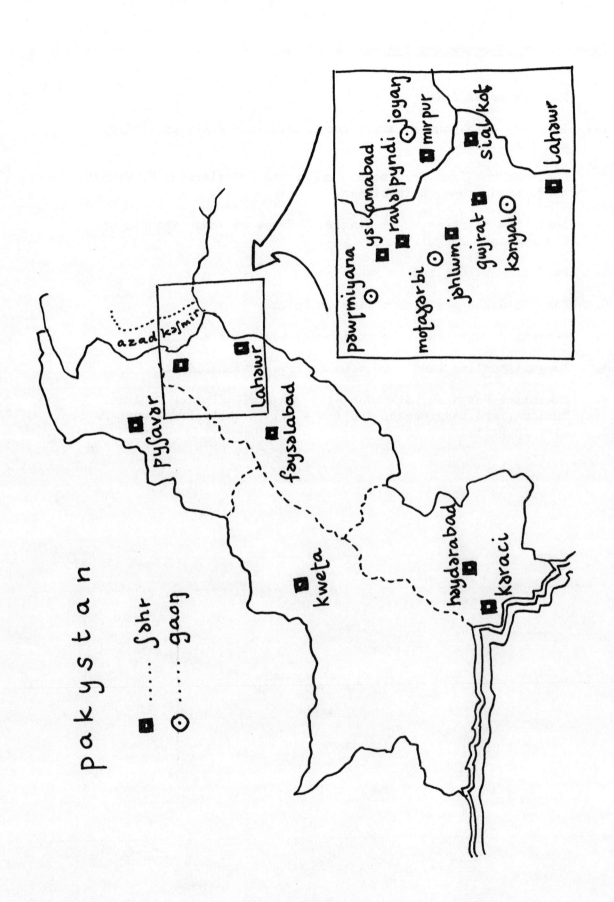

4.2 Pakistan

Look at the map on the page facing this one and listen to these sentences, reading them as you do so:

10. yyh pakystan həy.

11. pakystan ke car sube həyŋ.

12. azad kəʃmir bhi pakystan ke pas həy.

13. pyʃavər sərhəd ka bəɽa ʃəhr həy.

14. kveʈa bəlucystan ka bəɽa ʃəhr həy.

15. kəraci əwr həydərabad syndh ke do bəɽe ʃəhr həyŋ. (ek bəɽa ʃəhr həydərabad bharət meŋ bhi həy.)

16. pənjab ke kəi bəɽe ʃəhr həyŋ. wn meŋ se pəɲc lahəwr, mwltan, fəysəlabad, jəhlwm əwr ravəlpynɖi həyŋ.

17. yslamabad ravəlpynɖi ke pas həy. yyh pakystan ka dar-wl-hwkumət[1] həy.

18. mirpur azad kəʃmir ka ek ʃəhr həy.

19. pakystan meŋ ʃəhr kəm həyŋ əwr gaoŋ bəhwt zyada həyŋ.

20. yslamabad ravəlpyndi ke pas həy, əwr lahəwr se bəhwt dur həy – do səw mil dur (tin səw kylamyʈər dur).

21. pakystan ke kwch gaoŋ yyh[2] həyŋ:

    pəwɽmiyana: yyh ravəlpynɖi ke pas həy.
    moʈaɣərbi: yyh jəhlwm ke qərib həy, əwr ravəlpynɖi se kafi dur.
    kənyal: yyh jəhlwm ke pas həy.

22. joyaŋ azad kəʃmir meŋ ek gaoŋ həy. yyh mirpur ke pas həy.

23. pəwɽmiyana kafi bəɽa gaoŋ həy. kənyal choʈa sa gaoŋ həy.

Notes on sentences 10-23

12. -ke pas - near - People also say -ke qərib. Both are equally common. Note the 'q' sound. It's like 'k' but made further back, with your mouth open wide.

13. bəɽa - big

    ʃəhr - town

---

1. H. rajdhani.
2. H. ye.

15. The sentence in brackets means: 'One big city Hyderabad is in India too' - i.e. There is a big city called Hyderabad in India too.

16. kəi - several. (Often, incorrectly, used by Panjabis to mean 'many'.)

   wn men se panc - 'them in from 5' - i.e. out of them 5, 5 of them.

17. dar-wl-hwkumət[1] - 'place of government', capital.

19. kəm - less, few

   gaon - village

   zyada - more, many

   bəhwt zyada - very many

20. -se dur - far from -

   səw - hundred

   mil - mile

   tin - three

   kylamytər - kilometre(s)

21. Note the retroflex ṛ of pəwṛmiyana.

   Note the ɣ sound of motaɣərbi.

23. kafi - 'enough' - i.e. quite

   choṭa - small

   choṭa sa - 'smallish', quite small

Translation of sentences 10-23

10. This is Pakistan.

11. Pakistan has four provinces.

12. Azad Kashmir too is near Pakistan.

13. Peshawar is the Frontier's big city.

14. Quetta is Baluchistan's big city.

---

1.   H. rajdhani.

15. Karachi and Hyderabad are Sind's two big cities.   (One big
city Hyderabad is in India too.)

16. Panjab has several big cities.   Five of them are Lahore,
Multan, Faisalabad, Jhelum, and Rawalpindi.

17. Islamabad is near Rawalpindi.   This is the capital of Pakistan.

18. Mirpur is a city of Azad Kashmir.

19. In Pakistan cities are few and villages very many.

20. Islamabad is near Rawalpindi, and very far from Lahore - two
hundred miles far (three hundred kilometers far).

21. Some of Pakistan's villages are these:

      Paurmiyana: this is near Rawalpindi.

      Motagharbi: this is near Jhelum, and quite far from
          Rawalpindi.

      Kanyal: this is near Jhelum.

22. Joyan is a village of Azad Kashmir.   This is near Mirpur.

23. Paurmiyana is quite a big village.   Kanyal is a smallish village.

If you're being taught in a class your teachers will be questioning
you about the things you have learnt from the maps and the sentences about
them.   So you'll need to understand the question words:

kys mwlk[1] meŋ?   In what country?

kys sube meŋ?   In what province?

kys riyasət[2] meŋ?   In what state?

kytne sube?   How many provinces?

kytni riyasəteŋ?[3]   How many states?

---

1.   H. deʃ.
2.   H. prədeʃ.
3.   H. kytne prədeʃ.

<u>kytni</u> dur?	How far? Literally, How much far[ness]? – <u>kytni</u> can mean 'how much' as well as 'how many'.
<u>kytne</u> mil dur?	How many miles far?
<u>kytne</u> kylamyʈər?	How many kilometres?

4.3 Back to U.K.

Now listen to the following dialogue, reading as you listen:

24. A.   <u>June</u>, ap <u>Oxford</u> meŋ rəhti həyŋ?

25. J.   ji haŋ, məyŋ <u>Oxford</u> meŋ rəhti huŋ.

26. A.   <u>Oxford</u> bəɽa ʃəhr həy?

27. J.   ji haŋ, <u>Oxford</u> kafi bəɽa ʃəhr həy.

28. A.   ap <u>Oxford</u> meŋ kəhaŋ rəhti həyŋ?

29. J.   məyŋ <u>Cowley</u> meŋ rəhti huŋ.

30. A.   <u>John</u>, ap bhi <u>Oxford</u> meŋ rəhte həyŋ?

31. J.   ji nəhiŋ.   məyŋ <u>Kirtlington</u> meŋ rəhta huŋ.

32. A.   əccha?   <u>Kirtlington</u> ʃəhr həy, ya gaoŋ?

33. J.   <u>Kirtlington</u> gaoŋ həy.

34. A.   bəɽa gaoŋ həy?

35. J.   ji nəhiŋ, choʈa sa gaoŋ həy.

36. A.   <u>Kirtlington</u> kysi ʃəhr ke pas həy?

37. J.   ji haŋ, <u>Oxford</u> ke pas həy.

38. A.   <u>Oxford</u> se kytne mil dur həy?

39. J.   koi chəy mil dur həy – paŋc chəy mil.

40. A.   <u>ləndən</u> <u>Oxford</u> se kytne mil dur həy?

41. J.   <u>ləndən</u> <u>Oxford</u> se pəcas mil dur həy.

42. A.   əwr kytne kylamyʈər?

43. J.   mwjhe malum nəhiŋ – yad nəhiŋ.

---

1.   H. kytne prədeʃ.

Notes on sentences 24-43

32. Note the word order, with the hey before the ya gaoŋ. This is the regular order in Urdu/Hindi, and the only correct one!

36. kysi - you had this meaning 'someone' in Unit 1. It means not only that but 'some', or (as here) 'any'.

39. chey - six. Note that 'koi chey' means 'about 6'. Note also that Urdu/Hindi says not 'five to six miles' but 'five six miles'.

41. pecas - 50.

43. In case you need reminding, this sentence means

        'To me known not - remembered not'
   i.e.   I don't know - don't remember

English translation of sentences 24-43

24. A.   June, do you live in Oxford?

25. J.   Yes, I live in Oxford.

26. A.   Is Oxford a big city?

27. J.   Yes, Oxford's quite a big city.

28. A.   Where in Oxford do you live?

29. J.   I live in Cowley.

30. A.   John, do you too live in Oxford?

31. J.   No. I live in Kirtlington.

32. A.   Yes?   Is Kirtlington a town or a village?

33. J.   Kirtlington's a village.

34. A.   Is it a big village?

35. J.   No, it's quite a small village.

36. A.   Is Kirtlington near a ['some'] town?

37. J.   Yes, it's near Oxford.

38. A.   How many miles ['how many miles far'] from Oxford is it?

39. J. About six miles [far] - five or six miles.

40. A. How far is London from Oxford?

41. J. London is fifty miles from Oxford.

42. A. And how many kilometres?

43. J. I don't know - don't remember.

To follow unit 4

1. Q.   pakystan ke kytne sube həyŋ?

2. W/M.   pakystan ke car sube həyŋ.

3. Q.   pənjab ke do bəɽe ʃəhr bətaiye.

4. W/M.   lahəwr, ravəlpyndi. mwltan, fəysəlabad əwr jəhlwm bhi
   pənjab ke bəɽe ʃəhr həyŋ.

5. Q.   pənjab ka ek gaoŋ moṭaɣərbi həy. moṭaɣərbi ravəlpyndi
   ke qərib həy?

6. W/M.   ji nəhiŋ.   moṭaɣərbi ravəlpyndi se kafi dur həy.
   jəhlwm ke qərib həy.

7. Q.   azad kəʃmir kəhaŋ həy?

8. W/M.   azad kəʃmir pakystan ke pas həy.

9. Q.   ləndən Oxford se kytne mil dur həy?

10. W/M.   ləndən Oxford se pəcas mil dur həy.

Unit 5.   Work

Listen to, and then listen again, reading as you do so, the
dialogue on the page that follows this one.   In the first 19
sentences there are only two words that you haven't already met -

kam, which means 'work'

and the various forms

kərta, kərti, kərte, all of which mean 'do, does'.

(Mind you pronounce the r.)

In Urdu/Hindi idiom 'to work' is 'to do work', and kərti/kərta hun,
kərti/kərte hayn operate in exactly the same way as rəhti/rəhta hun,
rəhti/rəhte hayn.   As an exercise, take as many as you like of the
sentences of Lesson 3 and substitute in each of them kam kərti/kam
kərta/kam kərte as appropriate.   You will see that they will all mean
'work(s)' instead of 'live(s)'.

After you've read these sentences you should be able to write
and speak a few continuous sentences about yourself, saying what your
name is, where you live, and what work you do.   You should keep on
doing this from now on throughout the course, keeping in play all you've
learnt, and progressively adding new things as you learn how to say them.

In the sentences from 20 onwards you can see how to give the same
sort of information about your father, mother, parents, husband and
wife.*   Note the words for these:

> valyd[1] - father
>
> valyda[2] - mother
>
> valydəyn[3] - parents
>
> ʃəwhər[4] - husband
>
> bivi[5] - wife

Note also that vwh[6] means 'he, she, they' when these refer to people
who are not present.   (Just as yyh really means 'this/these', vwh
really means 'that/those'.)

> ghər - home, house
>
> -ke bahər - outside-

---

1.   H. pyta ji.
2.   H. mata ji.
3.   H. mata pyta.
4.   H. pəti.
5.   H. pətni.
6.   H. plu. (courteous and real) ve.

*   But don't attempt names yet.   This involves a point of grammar
      you've not yet learnt.

1. A.   məyŋ ʈicər huŋ.   <u>Betty</u>, bətaiye, ap kya kam kərti həyŋ?

2. B.   məyŋ ɖakʈər huŋ.

3. A.   əwr <u>Terry</u>, ap?   ap kya kam kərte həyŋ?

4. T.   məyŋ pwlisməyn huŋ.

5. A.   ap kəhaŋ kam kərte həyŋ?

6. T.   məyŋ <u>Oxford</u> meŋ kam kərta huŋ.   əwr ap?   ap bhi <u>Oxford</u> meŋ kam kərti həyŋ?

7. A.   ji haŋ, məyŋ bhi <u>Oxford</u> meŋ kam kərti huŋ.   <u>Som</u>, bətaiye, [indicating <u>Ann</u>] yyh[1] kəhaŋ kam kərti həyŋ?

8. S.   yyh[1] <u>Reading</u> meŋ kam kərti həyŋ.

9. A.   əwr kya kam kərti həyŋ?

10. S.   mwjhe malum nəhiŋ.

11. A.   malum nəhiŋ?   ya <u>yad</u> nəhiŋ?

12. S.   yad nəhiŋ!

13. A.   puchiye!

14. S.   <u>Ann</u>, ap kya kam kərti həyŋ?

15. A.   məyŋ soʃəl vərkər huŋ.

16. S.   əwr <u>June</u>? ap?

17. J.   məyŋ bhi soʃəl vərkər huŋ.   məyŋ əwr <u>Ann</u> donoŋ soʃəl vərkər həyŋ.   ap kya kam kərte həyŋ?

18. S.   məyŋ berozgar[2] huŋ.

19. John.   həm bhi - məyŋ əwr <u>Tom</u> - berozgar[2] həyŋ.

20. mere valyd[3] <u>Cowley</u> meŋ kam kərte həyŋ.   vwh ynjyniyər həyŋ.

21. meri valyda[4] ghər meŋ kam kərti həyŋ.   ghər ke bahər kam nəhiŋ kərtiŋ.

22. mere valydəyn[5] donoŋ ʈicər həyŋ.

23. mere ʃəwhər[6] berozgar[2] həyŋ.

24. meri bivi[7] ek skul meŋ kam kərti həyŋ.

---

1.   H. ye.
2.   H. bekar, which is also commonly used in Urdu.
3.   H. pyta ji.
4.   H. mata ji.
5.   H. mata pyta.
6.   H. pəti.
7.   H. pətni.

53.

To follow unit 5

1. Q. (to W) ap kya kam kərti həyŋ?

2. W. məyŋ .... huŋ.

3. Q. əwr kəhaŋ kam kərti həyŋ?

4. W. məyŋ .... meŋ kam kərti huŋ.

5. Q. (to M) əwr ap?   ap kya kam kərte həyŋ?

6. M. məyŋ .... huŋ.

7. Q. əwr kəhaŋ kam kərte həyŋ?

8. M. məyŋ .... meŋ kam kərta huŋ.

(The next questions need to be asked by a questioner who knows
something about you.   Since you don't know yet how to say
such things as 'I'm not married', 'My father is dead', etc.
It's no good her/him asking someone (e.g.) what work her
husband does unless he knows that she <u>has</u> a husband.   So the
questioner must direct the questions to those who he knows
can answer them with the sentences they have learnt.)

9. Q. ap ke valyd[1] kya kam kərte həyŋ?

10. W/M. mere valyd[1] .... həyŋ.

11. Q. əwr ap ki valyda?[2]

12. W/M. meri valyda[2].... həyŋ.

> <u>or</u>
>
> meri valyda[2] ghər ke bahər kam nəhiŋ kərti həyŋ (<u>or</u>, kərtiŋ*).
> ghər meŋ kam kərti həyŋ.

13. Q. (to W) ap ke ʃəwhər[3] kya kam kərte həyŋ?

14. W. mere ʃəwhər[3] .... həyŋ.

15. Q. (to M) ap ki bivi[4] ghər ke bahər kam kərti həyŋ?

16. M. ji həŋ; .... həyŋ

> <u>or</u>
>
> ji nəhiŋ, ghər meŋ kam kərti həyŋ.

---

1. H. pyta ji.
2. H. mata ji.
3. H. pəti.
4. H. pətni.

* See page 34.

Unit 6.   Sons and daughters

For this unit, you'll need to remind yourself of the numbers 1 to 6.

<u>ek</u>, <u>do</u>, <u>tin</u>, <u>car</u>, <u>paŋc</u>, <u>chəy</u>

You'll also need to understand the sentence

<u>təsvir nəmbər do ko dekhiye</u>

<u>təsvir</u> means 'picture'

<u>dekhiye</u> means 'see, look at'

-<u>ko</u> is a postposition which (here) doesn't mean anything - or to be more precise, in this sentence it doesn't correspond to any English <u>word</u>.   It just shows that 'təsvir nəmbər do' is the object of the sentence.

Other words you'll need to understand are:

<u>yn ka</u>, <u>yn ke</u> - in these sentences these words mean 'their'.   You know that in other contexts they can mean 'his' or 'her'.

<u>koi</u> - any

<u>beʈa</u> - son

<u>beʈe</u> - sons

<u>ʃadi-ʃwda</u> - married

For the present, these notes are enough.   I'll add others when you've heard the dialogue on page 56 .   You'll need at the same time to keep an eye on the pictures facing it.

Now do that.

1.

yn ka ek beʈa hɘy.

2.

yn ke do beʈe hɘyŋ.

3.

yn ka koi beʈa nɘhiŋ.

6.1 Sons

1. A.   Terry, təsvir nəmbər ek ko dekhiye əwr bətaiye, yn ka koi
         beţa həy?

2. T.   ji haŋ, yn ka ek beţa həy.

3. A.   ţhik həy. ʃabaʃ. June, ap təsvir nəmbər do ko dekhiye.
         yn ka koi beţa həy?

4. J.   ji haŋ, yn ke do beţe həyŋ.

5. A.   ţhik həy, yn ke do beţe həyŋ. Ann, təsvir nəmbər tin
         ko dekhiye.   yn ka koi beţa həy?

6. Ann ji nəhiŋ, yn ka koi beţa nəhiŋ.

7. A.   Terry, bətaiye, ap ʃadi-ʃwda həyŋ?

8. T.   ji haŋ, ʃadi-ʃwda huŋ.

9. A.   ap ka koi beţa həy?

10. T.   ji haŋ, mere tin beţe həyŋ.

11. A.   June, bətaiye, ap ʃadi-ʃwda həyŋ?

12. J.   ji nəhiŋ, məyŋ ʃadi-ʃwda nəhiŋ.

13. A.   Terry ʃadi-ʃwda həyŋ?

14. J.   ji haŋ, Terry ʃadi-ʃwda həyŋ.

15. A.   Terry ke kytne beţe həyŋ?

16. J.   mwjhe yad nəhiŋ. Terry, ap ke kytne beţe həyŋ?

17. T.   mere tin beţe həyŋ.

18. J.   Terry ke tin beţe həyŋ.

Notes

   You'll have registered that the sentence you use to ask people
whether people have any sons means literally

         Their any son is?

(Note the singular.)

And the answers follow the same pattern.

Note the retroflex t̪ of be̱t̪a̱.

Note: yn ka̱ ek be̱t̪a̱ həy.

yn ke̱ do be̱t̪e̱ həyŋ

Note in sentence 8 that mə̱yŋ can be omitted.

Now turn over the page.   Look at page   59, and at the pictures facing it, and follow the same instructions as you did for sentences 1-18.

4.  yn ki ek beţi həy.

 5.  yn ki do beţiyaŋ həyŋ.

 6.  yn ki koi beţi nəhiŋ.

6.2 Daughters

19. A.   əb təsvir nəmbər car ko dekhiye.   <u>Tom</u>, ap bətaiye, yn ki
koi beṭi həy?

20. T.   ji haŋ, yn ki ek beṭi həy.

21. A.   ṭhik həy. ʃabaʃ. <u>Betty</u>, ap təsvir nəmbər paŋc ko dekhiye.
yn ki koi beṭi həy?

22. B.   ji haŋ, yn ki do beṭiyaŋ həyŋ.

23. A.   ji haŋ, yn ki do beṭiyaŋ həyŋ.   əb təsvir nəmbər chəy ko
dekhiye.   <u>Peter</u>, ap bətaiye, yn ki koi beṭi həy?

24. P.   ji nəhiŋ, yn ki koi beṭi nəhiŋ.

25. A.   <u>Terry</u>, ap ʃadi-ʃwda həyŋ, əwr ap ke do beṭe həyŋ.

26. T.   mere <u>tin</u> beṭe həyŋ.

27. A.   ji haŋ, <u>tin</u> beṭe. mwaf[1] kijiye!   ap ki koi beṭi bhi həy?

28. T.   ji nəhiŋ, meri koi beṭi nəhiŋ.

29. A.   <u>Betty</u>, ap ʃadi-ʃwda həyŋ?

30. B.   ji haŋ, ʃadi-ʃwda huŋ.

31. A.   ap ka koi beṭa həy?

32. B.   ji nəhiŋ, mera koi beṭa nəhiŋ.   do beṭiyaŋ həyŋ.

33. A.   <u>Ann</u>, bətaiye, <u>Terry</u> ke kytne beṭe həyŋ, əwr <u>Betty</u> ki kytni
beṭiyaŋ?

34. Ann <u>Terry</u> ke tin beṭe həyŋ, əwr <u>Betty</u> ki do beṭiyaŋ həyŋ.

Note

You'll have guessed that <u>beṭi</u> means 'daughter' and <u>beṭiyaŋ</u>
'daughters'.

   Note: yn k<u>i</u> ek beṭi həy

          yn k<u>i</u> do beṭiyaŋ həyŋ.

(Notice how we spell <u>beṭiyaŋ</u>.   Those of you who later learn the
Devanagari (Hindi) script will see the point of this spelling then.
For the present there is no need to explain it.   And the spelling
<u>beṭiaŋ</u> is also acceptable.)

---

1.   or, <u>maf</u>, which is the standard pronunciation in H.   H. also
     says k<u>ʃ</u>əma.

27. <u>mwaf</u>[1] <u>kijiye</u>, as you've probably guessed, means 'Sorry', 'Excuse mē', 'I beg your pardon', etc. (But Urdu/Hindi speakers use it much less profusely than English speakers use 'sorry'.)

33. Remember that <u>kytne?</u> means 'how many?'   This sentence shows you that for feminines you say <u>kytni?</u>

6.3 <u>Children</u>

Now listen to this dialogue:

35. A.   <u>nəsim</u>, ap ∫adi-∫wda həyŋ?

36. N.   ji haŋ, ∫adi-∫wda huŋ.

37. A.   bəcce bhi həyŋ?

38. N.   ji haŋ.   bəcce bhi həyŋ.

39. A.   kytne?

40. N.   car bəcce həyŋ.

41. A.   ləɽke?   ya ləɽkiyaŋ?   ya donoŋ?

42. N.   donoŋ - ek ləɽka əwr tin ləɽkiyaŋ.

43. A.   <u>gwlzar</u>, ap ∫adi-∫wda həyŋ?

44. G.   ji haŋ, ∫adi-∫wda huŋ - bəcce nəhiŋ həyŋ.

45. A.   əwr <u>June</u>?   ap ∫adi-∫wda həyŋ.   ap ke bəcce bhi həyŋ?

46. J.   ji haŋ, car bəcce həyŋ.   caroŋ ləɽke həyŋ.

<u>Notes</u>

<u>bəcce</u> means 'children'.   Note the doubling of the 'c'.

<u>ləɽka</u> - boy

<u>ləɽke</u> - boys

<u>ləɽki</u> - girl

<u>ləɽkiyaŋ</u> - girls

---

1.   or, <u>maf</u>, which is the standard pronunciation in H.   H. also says k∫əma.

42. Notice that Nasim answers that she has both boys and girls, and goes on to specify how many of each.

It's easiest to answer in this way, so that the answer specifies boys and girls. The reason for this is that <u>bəcca</u> (the singular of <u>bəcce</u>) is not the strict equivalent of the English word 'child', which can refer either to a boy or girl. <u>bəcca</u> means 'boy', and 'girl' is <u>bəcci</u>. You can use the masculine plural form in asking

    bəcce bhi həyŋ?

because you don't know whether the children, if any, are boys or girls or both, and <u>bəcce</u> is alright in this situation.

The reply

    ji haŋ, bəcce bhi həyŋ

is O.K. for the same reason - provided that at least one of them is a boy, because the masculine plural form covers both masculine and mixed genders.

Where you absolutely need a word that means 'child' without specifying its gender, you can, in Urdu, use <u>əwlad</u>.[1] This is a feminine singular noun, and means 'progeny', though it doesn't sound so high-flown in Urdu as 'progeny' does in English. But it is used to mean 'child' as well. So you could say, e.g.

    bəɾi əwlad[1] ləɾka həy ya ləɾki?
    Is the big (i.e. eldest) child a boy or a girl?

Anyway, if your answer to the question <u>kytne</u>? already specifies how many boys and how many girls you have, you avoid this difficulty altogether.

44. <u>caroŋ</u> means 'all four', just as <u>donoŋ</u> means 'all two', i.e. both. You can stick this <u>-oŋ</u> ending on <u>any</u> number to give the same sense.

    <u>tinoŋ</u> - all three

    <u>pəɲcoŋ</u> - all five

---

1. H. <u>səntən</u> (f.). But this is rarely used in the <u>spoken</u> language.

To follow unit 6

1. Q.   ap ʃadi-ʃwda həyŋ?

2. W/M.   ji nəhiŋ, məyŋ ʃadi-ʃwda nəhiŋ huŋ.

    <u>or</u>

    ji haŋ, [məyŋ] ʃadi-ʃwda huŋ.

3. Q.   ap ka koi beʈa həy?

4. W/M.   ji nəhiŋ, mera koi beʈa nəhiŋ.

    <u>or</u>

    ji haŋ, mera ek beʈa həy.

    <u>or</u>

    ji haŋ mere [do, tin...] beʈe həyŋ.

5. Q.   koi beʈi həy?

6. W/M.   ji nəhiŋ, meri koi beʈi nəhiŋ.

    <u>or</u>

    ji haŋ, meri ek beʈi həy.

    <u>or</u>

    ji haŋ, meri [do, tin...] beʈiyaŋ həyŋ.

7. Q.   ap ke kytne bəcce həyŋ?

8. W/M.   mera koi bəcca nəhiŋ.

    <u>or</u>

    mere .... bəcce həyŋ

    <u>or</u>

    mera koi bəcca nəhiŋ;   ek bəcci həy.

    <u>or</u>

    mera koi bəcca nəhiŋ .... bəcciyaŋ həyŋ.

Unit 7.   Brothers and Sisters

7.1   Sisters

Look at the pictures, and the dialogue facing them, on the next two pages, and do the same as you did in Unit 6.

You will need to know that

bəhyn means 'sister'

bəhyneŋ means 'sisters'

choṭi means 'little' - and in this context (as often in English) means 'younger'

bəṛi means 'big' - and in this context (as often in English) means 'elder'.

The rest ought to be clear to you.   I shall add one or two notes after you've done this exercise.

1.  nəsim ki ek bəhyn həyŋ.

2.  rəzia ki do bəhyneŋ həyŋ.

3. 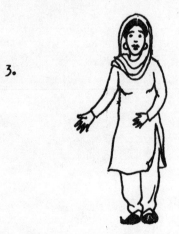 fatyma ki koi bəhyn nəhiŋ.

1. A.   təsvir nəmbər ek ko dekhiye, əwr...<u>Ken</u>, ap bətaiye,
   <u>nəsim</u> ki koi bəhyn həy?

2. K.   ji haŋ, <u>nəsim</u> ki ek bəhyn həyŋ.

3. A.   ʈhik həy, <u>nəsim</u> ki ek bəhyn həyŋ. əb təsvir nəmbər tin
   ko dekhiye. <u>fatyma</u> ki koi bəhyn həy?

4. K.   ji nəhiŋ, <u>fatyma</u> ki koi bəhyn nəhiŋ.

5. A.   əb təsvir nəmbər do ko dekhiye. <u>rəzia</u> ki koi bəhyn həy?

6. K.   ji haŋ, <u>rəzia</u> ki do bəhyneŋ həyŋ.

7. A.   əwr ap? ap ki koi bəhyn həy?

8. K.   ji haŋ, meri tin bəhyneŋ həyŋ.

9. A.   <u>Jill</u>, bətaiye. [Pointing to Sue] yn ki koi bəhyn həy?

10. J.   mwjhe malum nəhiŋ. <u>Sue</u>, ap ki koi bəhyn həy?

11. S.   ji haŋ, meri bhi tin bəhyneŋ həyŋ.

12. A.   <u>Sue</u>, <u>Jill</u> ki koi bəhyn həy?

13. S.   mwjhe malum nəhiŋ. <u>Jill</u>, ap ki koi bəhyn həy?

14. J.   ji haŋ, meri ek bəhyn həy - ek choʈi bəhyn.

15. A.   əwr <u>Ann</u>, ap ki koi bəhyŋ həy?

16. Ann   ji haŋ, meri ek bəhyn həyŋ.

17. A.   ek bəhyn həyŋ, ya ek bəhyŋ həy?

18. Ann   ek bəhyn həyŋ. vwh[1] meri bəɽi bəhyn həyŋ.

Notes

Note the variations in these sentences between <u>həy</u> and <u>həyŋ</u>.

You already know that <u>həyŋ</u> may be a real plural or a courteous one,
and that the courteous one is used when you are speaking to, or about,
people whom you regard as your equals, seniors or superiors. In these
sentences the Urdu/Hindi convention about age is exemplified. You <u>must</u>
use the plural of your older sibling, even if (s)he is only a year
older. And, in general, you <u>must</u> use the singular of your younger
sibling. So, in sentence 14 the listener knows at once from the verb
that the sister is a younger one, and in sentence 16 (verified in the
question and answer in 17-18) that the sister is an elder one.

---

1.   H. ve.

When you're <u>asking</u> 'Your any sister is?' - i.e. have you any sisters?, clearly the question of status - elder or younger - doesn't arise.   The 'sister' you're asking about may not even exist, and if she does you don't know yet what her status is.   So the verb is <u>hey</u>.

Note also that if you address me as <u>ap</u> and speak of me as <u>yyh</u>,[1] with a plural verb, you are likely to put my sisters - older or younger - in the same category as me.

<u>I</u> will use the singular for my younger sister, but it doesn't follow that <u>you</u> would.

You'll be learning more about these things in the next unit.

---

1.   H. ye.

4.    nəsim ke ek bhai həyŋ.

5.    rəzia ke do bhai həyŋ.

6.    kəniz ka koi bhai nəhiŋ.

7.2   Brothers

Here is a parallel exercise about brothers. As before, keep
both the pictures and the facing dialogue before you, and listen to,
and read, the dialogue.

19. A.   təsvir nəmbər car ko dekhiye, əwr bətaiye - Terry, ap
          bətaiye, nəsim ka koi bhai həy?

20. T.   ji haŋ, nəsim ke ek bhai həyŋ.

21. A.   ʈhik həy. əb təsvir nəmbər chəy ko dekhiye. kəniz
          ka koi bhai həy?

22. T.   ji nəhiŋ. kəniz ka koi bhai nəhiŋ.

23. A.   ʈhik həy. əb təsvir nəmbər pəŋc ko dekhiye. rəzia
          ke kytne bhai həyŋ?

24. T.   rəzia ke do bhai həyŋ.

25. A.   ji haŋ. əccha, Ken, ap ki kytni bəhyneŋ həyŋ? mwaf[1]
          kijiye, mwjhe yad nəhiŋ.

26. K.   meri tin bəhyneŋ həyŋ.

27. A.   əccha, tin bəhyneŋ. ap ka koi bhai bhi həy?

28. K.   ji haŋ, mera ek bhai həy.

29. A.   ap ka ek bhai həy? ya ap ke ek bhai həyŋ?

30. K.   mera ek bhai həy - ek choʈa bhai.

Notes

As you see, questions and answers about brothers run closely
parallel to questions and answers about sisters, with the same variations
between həy and həyŋ. In this respect there's one difference however.

The ki of yn ki, ap ki, nəsim ki doesn't vary. ki goes with the
singular, the courteous plural, and the real plural alike, since this
is the form for all feminines.

But with masculine singular you have ka, whereas for plurals (of
both kinds) you have ke. You already met this variation in the first
part of Unit 6, about sons.

---

1.   H. maf, or kʃəma.

So also <u>choṭi</u> and <u>bəṛi</u> go with feminines.

<u>choṭa</u> and <u>bəṛa</u> with masculine singulars.

and <u>choṭe</u> and <u>bəṛe</u> with (courteous and real) masculine plurals.

It's worth noting here that many South Asians will say

> <u>həm chəy bhai bəhyn həyŋ</u>
> 'we six brothers-sisters are'
> i.e. We are six brothers and sisters

rather than

> '<u>I have</u> five brothers and sisters'

i.e. they will use a form of words which includes <u>them</u> in the count.
(Note also 'bhai bəhyn' as a collective masculine plural; you may also
hear 'bəhyn bhai' used in exactly the same way). You ask:

> <u>ap kytne bhai bəhyn həyŋ?</u>
> How many brothers-sisters are you?

Similarly they will often say

> <u>həm pəŋc bhai həyŋ</u>
>
> 'we five brothers are'
> i.e. We are five brothers

where we would say

> 'I have four brothers'

and <u>həm car bəhyneŋ həyŋ</u>
> 'we four sisters are'
> We are four sisters

where we would say

> 'I have three sisters'

Watch out for this. Because Urdu/Hindi speakers are used to expressing
things in this way they may well <u>register</u> 'How many brothers <u>are</u> you?'
when you have asked 'How many brothers <u>have</u> you?' and may answer
according to what they <u>think</u> you asked rather than what you <u>did</u> ask.
The reverse is also true. You have to listen carefully to what it is
<u>you</u> have been asked.

And this seems the appropriate place to tell you that people will commonly refer to their cousins as <u>bhai</u> or <u>bəhynen</u> as the case may be. (This derives from the experience of the extended family - ask your teachers to explain how.) Your 'real brothers' - i.e. brothers in the English sense of the word - (and many South Asians use this phrase, which is a straight translation from Urdu/Hindi) are your

<u>səge bhai</u> or <u>həqiqi bhai</u>[1]

and your 'real sisters' are your

<u>səgi bəhynen</u> or <u>həqiqi bəhynen</u>[1]

An only daughter would say

<u>məyn ykləwti bet̪i hun</u>
'I only daughter am'
I am an only daughter

and an only son would say

<u>məyn ykləwta bet̪a hun</u>
I am an only son

If you want to say 'I am an only <u>child</u>', you would say:

<u>məyn ykləwti əwlad[2] hun</u>
I am an only child

Remember, you met 'əwlad' in unit 6.

---

1. H. has only səga, -i, -e - not həqiqi.
2. H. səntən.

To follow unit 7.2

1. Q.   ap ki koi bəhyn həy?

2. W/M.   ji nəhiŋ, meri koi bəhyn nəhiŋ.

          or

          ji haŋ, meri ek choṭi bəhyn həy

          or

          ji haŋ, meri ek bəṛi bəhyn həyŋ.

          or

          ji haŋ, meri .... bəhyneŋ həyŋ.

3. Q.   ap ka koi bhai həy?

4. W/M.   ji nəhiŋ, mera koi bhai nəhiŋ.

          or

          ji haŋ, mera ek choṭa bhai həy.

          or

          ji haŋ, mere ek bəṛe bhai həyŋ.

          or

          ji haŋ, mere .... bhai həyŋ.

5. Q.   (to W) ap ykləwti əwlad[1] həyŋ?

6. W.   ji haŋ, ykləwti əwlad[1] huŋ.

          or

          ji nəhiŋ. həm .... bhai bəhyn həyŋ.

          or

          ji nəhiŋ, həm .... bəhyneŋ həyŋ.

          or

          ji nəhiŋ, ykləwti əwlad[1] nəhiŋ huŋ. ykləwti beṭi huŋ.

[Then:]

          mera ek bhai həy.

              or

          mere ek bhai həyŋ.

              or

          mere .... bhai həyŋ.

---

1.   H. səntən.

7.   Q.   (to M) ap ykləwti əwlad[1] həyŋ?

8.   M.   ji haŋ, ykləwti əwlad[1] huŋ.

　　　　　　　　_or_

　　　　ji nəhiŋ, həm .... bhai bəhyn həyŋ.

　　　　　　　　_or_

　　　　ji nəhiŋ, həm .... bhai həyŋ.

　　　　　　　　_or_

　　　　ji nəhiŋ, ykləwti əwlad nəhiŋ huŋ. ykləwta beṭa huŋ.

[Then:]

　　　　　meri ek choṭi bəhyn həy.

　　　　　　　　_or_

　　　　　meri ek bəṛi bəhyn həyŋ.

　　　　　　　　_or_

　　　　　meri .... bəhyneŋ həyŋ.

────────

1.   H. səntən.

You have now met an example of each of what can be described as the four classes of Urdu/Hindi nouns:

1. Masculine nouns ending in -a, e.g. beta.

2. Masculine nouns not ending in -a, e.g. bhai.

3. Feminine nouns ending in -i, e.g. beti.

4. Feminine nouns not ending in -i, e.g. bahyn.

Some adjectives have only one form, regardless of the gender or number of the noun they go with - e.g.

> haqiqi bhai
>
> haqiqi bahyn
>
> haqiqi bahynen

Others have endings that change according to the gender and number of the nouns they go with

> ek choti bahyn
>
> do choti bahynen
>
> ek chota bhai
>
> do chote bhai

You have also seen how the nouns of each class form their plural.

1. Masculine nouns ending in -a form the plural by changing a to -e, e.g. do bete.

2. Masculine nouns not ending in -a have a plural form which is the same as the singular, e.g. do bhai.

3. Feminine nouns ending in -i form the plural by adding -an, e.g. do betiyan. (Note the spelling betiyan. The spelling betian is also acceptable).

4. Feminine nouns not ending in i form the plural by adding -en, e.g. do bahynen.

All these forms are set out for you in the table below, where I give just one example of each.

Forms of noun and agreement of adjectives

	Singular	Plural
masc. nouns in -a	mera (ek) beṭa my (one) son	mere (do, tin...) beṭe my (2, 3...) sons
masc. nouns not in -a	mera (ek) bhai my (one) brother	mere (do, tin...) bhai my (2, 3...) brothers
fem. nouns in -i	meri (ek) beṭi my (one) daughter	meri (do, tin...) beṭiyaŋ my (2, 3...) daughters
fem. nouns not in -i	meri (ek) bəhyn my (one) sister	meri (do, tin...) bəhyneŋ my (2, 3...) sisters

You may be vaguely aware that you met some of these forms before you reached units 6 and 7. See if you can work out the answers to the questions on the next page from the general rules and the table you've just been given. I give the answers, printed upside down, at the bottom of the page.

7.3 Exercise on the singulars and plurals of nouns

1. In unit 1, sentence 10 you had <u>səb əwratəŋ</u>.[1] What will the Urdu/Hindi (hereafter U/H) for 'one woman' be?

2. In unit 1, sentence 11 you had <u>səb mərd</u>.[2] What will the U/H for 'one man' be?

3. In unit 4, sentence 2 you had <u>tin mwlk</u>.[3] What will the U/H for 'one country' be?

4. In unit 4, sentence 3 you had <u>car sube</u>. What will the U/H for 'one province' be?

5. In unit 4, sentence 4 you had <u>tera riyasəteŋ</u>.[4] What will the U/H for 'one state' be?

6. In unit 4, sentences 5-9 you had <u>mwsəlman</u>, <u>sykh</u>, <u>hyndu</u> meaning 'Muslims, Sikhs, and Hindus'. What will the U/H for 'one Muslim, one Sikh, and one Hindu' be?

7. In unit 4, sentence 13 you had <u>ek ʃəhr</u> (ʃəhr is masculine). What will the U/H for 'two cities' be?

8. In unit 4, sentence 23 you had [ek] <u>gaoŋ</u> (gaoŋ is masculine). What will the U/H for 'three villages' be?

9. <u>ʃəwhər</u>[5] means 'husband'. What is the U/H for 'husbands'?

10. <u>bivi</u>[6] means 'wife'. What is the U/H for 'wives'?

11. <u>təsvir</u> means 'picture'. It is feminine. What is the U/H for 'pictures'?

12. <u>ləɽke</u> means 'boys'. What is the U/H for 'boy'?

13. <u>ləɽki</u> means 'girl'. What is the U/H for 'girls'?

14. <u>bəcca</u> means '(male) child'. What is the U/H for 'children'?

15. <u>bəcciyaŋ</u> means '(female) children'. What is the U/H for '(female) child'?

---

1. H. or, striyəŋ.   3. H. deʃ.   5. H. pəti.
2. H. admi.   4. H. pradeʃ.   6. H. pətni.

---

1) ek əwrat. (H. stri). 2) ek mərd. 3) ek mwlk. 4) ek suba.
5) ek riyasət. 6) ek mwsəlman, ek sykh, əwr ek hyndu. 7) do ʃəhr.
8) tin gaoŋ. 9) ʃəwhar. 10) biviyaŋ. (H. pətniyaŋ) 11) təsvirəŋ.
12) ləɽka. 13) ləɽkiyaŋ. 14) bəcce 15) bəcci.

7.4   <u>Exercise on agreement of adjectives and possessives with their nouns.</u>

Now practice the way in which adjectives and possessives ('my, your, his, her, their', etc.) agree with the nouns they go with.   Here are sentences which are complete except for adjectives or possessives, and you have to complete each sentence by supplying the appropriate form of the adjective or possessive to fill the blank.   I shall give the adjective/possessive in brackets at the end of the sentence in its masculine singular form.   Where necessary you must change it to the form needed in the sentence in question. So I shall write (e.g.)

      June......beʈi həy (wn ka)

and you have to work out that the sentence will be

      June wn ki beʈi həy.

and write it out in full.   Be sure you think about what each sentence means as you do this!

In most cases either the meaning or the form of the noun tells you whether it is masculine or feminine.   Where you <u>can't</u> tell, I give you the gender - m. for masculine and f. for feminine - in brackets after it.

Only one of the sentences uses a word you haven't already met in previous units.   You may find it useful to look back at the sentences in unit 4.

Remember that only adjectives whose masculine singular ends in -<u>a</u> change their forms.   Others - e.g. pakystani, sykh - remain unchanged.   The ones in -<u>a</u> change as follows:

masculine singular   bəɽa becomes bəɽe ⎫
                chota   "   choʈe ⎬ to agree with a masculine
                mera   "   mere   ⎬ plural noun
                yn ka   "   yn ke ⎬
                ap ka   "   ap ke ⎭

The feminine form that goes with <u>all</u> feminine nouns, whether singular or plural ends in -<u>i</u>.

      bəɽi
      choʈi
      meri
      yn ki
      ap ki

Here are the sentences:

1. bharət ek bəhwt _____ mwlk[1] (m.) həy.   (bəɽa)

2. pakystan əwr bangladeʃ bhi bəhwt _____ mwlk[1] həyŋ.   (bəɽa)

3. məyŋ _____ əwlad[2] (f.) huŋ.   (ykləwta)

4. _____ car beţe həyŋ.   (yn ka)

5. wn ka _____ bhai Reading meŋ kam kərta həy.   (choţa)

6. _____ donoŋ beţiyəŋ ţicər həyŋ.   (mera)

7. pakystan meŋ _____ sube həyŋ?   (kytna)

8. bharət meŋ tera _____ riyasəteŋ həyŋ.[3]   (bəɽa)

9. _____ biviyəŋ[4] ghər ke bahər kam nəhiŋ kərtiŋ.   (yn ka)

10. kənyal kafi _____ gaoŋ (m.) həy.   (choţa)

11. bəlucystan ek bəhwt _____ suba həy.   (bəɽa)

12. lahəwr əwr kəraci donoŋ _____ ʃəhr (m.) həyŋ.   (bəɽa)

13. _____ ləɽke ləndən meŋ kam kərte həyŋ.   (choţa)

14. _____ donoŋ beţe yslamabad meŋ həyŋ?   (ap ka)

15. _____ ek beţi Oxford meŋ rəhti həy.   (wn ka)

16. _____ beţa ţicər həy.   (mera)

17. pəwɽmiyana əwr moţaɣərbi kafi _____ gaoŋ (m.) həyŋ.   (bəɽa)

18. kveţa bəhwt _____ ʃəhr (m.) nəhiŋ həy.   (bəɽa)

19. donoŋ bəhyneŋ kafi _____ həyŋ.

    (ləmba - ləmba means 'long', or, as in this context, 'tall')

20. _____ car bhai həyŋ.   (mera)

---

1. H. deʃ.
2. H. səntən (f.).
3. H. prədeʃ (m.).
4. H. pətniyəŋ.

Unit 8.   Status and courtesy

Look at the first four sentences below, and at the English meaning of each one:

<u>mera nam Ralph həy.</u>
My name is Ralph.

<u>məyŋ Ralph huŋ.</u>
I am Ralph.

<u>məyŋ London meŋ rəhta huŋ.</u>
I live in London.

<u>məyŋ Burton meŋ rəhti huŋ.</u>
I live in Burton.

In all these sentences the subject is a single person or a single thing, and the verb forms – həy, huŋ, rəhta huŋ, rəhti huŋ – are singular.   In the next five sentences given below, the subjects are in every case more than one person – i.e. plural – and the verb forms are plural:

məyŋ əwr June əwr Ken ţicər <u>həyŋ.</u>
June and Ken and I are teachers.

həm Burton meŋ <u>rəhte həyŋ.</u>
We live in Burton.

həm – Margaret əwr Jill – donoŋ Burton meŋ <u>rəhte</u>[1] həyŋ.
We – Margaret and Jill – both live in Burton.

rəʃida əwr əziza Princess Street meŋ <u>rəhti həyŋ.</u>
Rashida and Aziza live in Princess Street.

rəʃida əwr əli Park Street meŋ <u>rəhte həyŋ.</u>
Rashida and Ali live in Park Street.

Note that həyŋ, rəhte həyŋ and rəhti həyŋ are all plurals.

But you've seen that we have used these same plural forms in speaking of single people.   For example:

yyh[2] Margaret <u>həyŋ.</u>
means This <u>is</u> Margaret.

---

1.   H. (and many Panjabi speakers) rəhti.
2.   H. ye.

Margaret Burton meŋ <u>rəhti həyŋ</u>.
means Margaret lives in Burton.

Ken Yoxall meŋ <u>rəhte həyŋ</u>.
means Ken lives in Yoxall.

In Urdu/Hindi these plural forms are used as a mark of courtesy. (I first touched on this in Unit 3. Now I am spelling it out more fully.) We do it in English too, usually without realising that we're doing it. 'You' is really a plural form, and it can be a <u>real</u> plural. If you hear someone saying 'Where are you going?' and can't see who he's speaking to, you can't tell whether the 'you' is one person or more than one. But you use the plural form in either case. 'Are' is a plural form. You can't say 'Where <u>is</u> you going?' - using the singular form 'is'. And you can't use the old English singular 'Where art thou going?'.

What English does in the second person ('you') Urdu/Hindi does in the third persons (he, she, they) too, and the general rule is that when you are speaking to, or about, people of equal, or senior, or superior status to yourself you <u>must</u> use the plural forms for them. That's why I say

Margaret Burton meŋ <u>rəhti həyŋ</u>

- because Margaret is my equal.

This is perhaps the point at which to tell you that in South Asian society people have (to an English way of thinking) a very rigid and very complex sense of status. The tradition might be described as 'A place for everyone, and everyone in his or her place'. This is best illustrated by the fact that in good Urdu/Hindi you have <u>three</u> words that mean 'you' - <u>ap</u>, <u>twm</u> and <u>tu</u>.

<u>ap</u>

is for equals, seniors, and superiors, and this is the 'you' which you will have most occasion to use. That's why in this course we shall concentrate on <u>ap</u> and on the forms that go with it.

<u>twm</u>

you will also have occasion both to hear and to use. If you were an Urdu/Hindi speaker you could address your children as <u>twm</u>, and you could also use it for your close friends. If you're a teacher, practising your Urdu/Hindi on Urdu/Hindi-speaking boys and girls in your school, some may expect you to call them <u>twm</u>, and not <u>ap</u>. But you'll find that different people have different conventions. Many parents will address <u>young</u> children as <u>ap</u>, so that the children learn to call <u>them</u> 'ap'. Many teachers will also call older children '<u>ap</u>'. But '<u>twm</u>' will be regularly used by others in addressing children between the ages of, say, 11 and 16.

tu

is for very young children, or for people whom you treat either with
very great intimacy, or with marked superiority and/or contempt. It's
use is decreasing now, and although you may hear it, it's most unlikely
that you'll ever have occasion to speak it. (tu is also used in
addressing God.)

Each 'you' has its own appropriate accompanying forms. You have
already met the ap forms in, for example

ap kəhaŋ rəhti həyŋ?

for addressing a woman, or women, and

ap kəhaŋ rəhte həyŋ?

for addressing a man, or men.

The appropriate twm forms are:

twm kəhaŋ rəhti ho?

for addressing a female twm person or persons, and

twm kəhaŋ rəhte ho?

for a male twm person or persons.

The courteous plurals are used to refer to, or to address, someone
of ap status, i.e. someone of equal, senior, or superior status, whom
you would address as ap. The singular is used to refer to someone of
twm status, i.e. someone subordinate or junior in status, whom you would
address as twm. (The table at the end of this unit will set all this
out.)

Before I tell you about other verb forms, let me explain a few
terms I shall use in talking about the verb.

If you look up an Urdu/Hindi verb in a dictionary, what is given
there is the infinitive. This always ends in -na and can usually be
translated (e.g.) to say, to ask, etc.

kəhna	to say
puchna	to ask
swnna	to listen

The root (some books call it the stem) is the infinitive minus the
-na.

Infinitive:	kəhna
Root:	kəh

Infinitive:	puchna
Root:	puch

Infinitive:	swnna
Root:	swn

For regular verbs, the imperative[*] is formed from the root:

root + -iye   for addressing an ap person

root + -o   for addressing a twm person

(The tu form of the imperative is the same as the root, e.g. telling a tu person to listen, you say swn.)

As you will remember, when you're telling an ap person to say something you say

kəhiye
(Please) say (it)

and the twm form is

kəho
say (it)

Telling an ap person to ask, you say

puchiye
(Please) ask

and the twm form is

pucho
(ask)

Telling an ap person to listen, you say

swniye
please listen

and the twm form is

swno
listen

In the ap, or courteous, form of the imperative, the respect is built in, making words such as 'please' unnecessary.

Many Panjabi speakers of Urdu say not kəhiye but kəheŋ, not swniye, but swneŋ. You'll meet this form in due course, but its use as an equivalent of the -iye form is not acceptable in standard Urdu/Hindi.

Some other useful imperatives are:

aiye (from ana, to come) - 'come', often where English would say 'please come in'

---

[*] This is the name of the form you use to tell, or ask, someone to do something.

<u>bəɣ</u>hiye (from <u>bəɣ</u>hna, to sit down) – sit down,
    take a seat)

pərhiye (from <u>pər</u>hna, to read) – read

People learning spoken Urdu/Hindi often ask how you say 'please' and 'thank you'. The answer is threefold.

First, you <u>can</u> say

<u>myhrbani kərke</u>[1]

which literally means 'doing kindness' – i.e. kindly, or please. And you <u>can</u> say 'ʃwkriya'[2] – which you met earlier (in unit 2) for 'Thank you'. (Many Panjabis will say, instead of 'ʃwkriya', 'myhrbani', kindness – i.e. 'It is kind of you', i.e. Thank you.)

But Urdu/Hindi speakers don't say Please and Thank you on every conceivable occasion as British people tend to do, but reserve these words for occasions when they really do feel that they are asking you for, and then expressing gratitude for, a real favour (cf. the note on <u>mwaf kijiye</u> in unit 6, sentence 27). So the second part of the answer is that very often <u>English</u> please and thank you don't <u>have</u> an Urdu/Hindi equivalent. It's important to realise that the frequency with which we say please and thank you is simply a <u>convention</u> – just as much a convention as their convention of <u>not</u> saying it so frequently. It doesn't imply any lower standard of courtesy on their part.

And the third part of the answer is that the force of please and thank you are conveyed partly by the tone and manner in which you speak and partly by the <u>form</u> you use. E.g. <u>swniye</u>, listen, is the form that goes with <u>ap</u> and <u>only</u> with <u>ap</u>, and therefore in itself implies the politeness which English 'please' expresses.

Having said all that let me add that most Urdu/Hindi speakers in Britain are Panjabis, who don't have Urdu/Hindi as their mother tongue and don't always speak it completely correctly. You will often find that with them, the <u>twm</u> and <u>ap</u> distinction sometimes gets a bit blurred at the edges. They will <u>sometimes</u> use <u>twm</u> where a person of Urdu/Hindi mother tongue would use <u>ap</u> and quite often use the <u>twm</u> verb-form with an <u>ap</u> pronoun. But these things won't hinder mutual comprehension in any way.

I said earlier on that the use of the plural for courtesy extends in Urdu/Hindi to the third person (he, she, they). It does, and there is another important distinction too that you have to observe in translating these pronouns into Urdu/Hindi. Sometimes they are to be translated by

<u>yyh</u>[4]

---

1. H. also, but less commonly, krypa kərke.
2. H. or, more formally, dhənyəvad.
3. H. maf, or kʃəma.
4. H. plu. ye.

And at other times the translation will be

vwh[1]

These two words really mean 'this' and 'that' respectively. 'yyh əwrət'[2] means 'this woman', and 'vwh əwrət'[2] means 'that woman'.

So when the he, she, or they of whom you're speaking is/are present, you generally say 'yyh'[3] and when they're <u>not</u> present, you say 'vwh'.[1]   But there are circumstances in which you would use vwh[1] of people present - for example in speaking of a group of people talking together elsewhere in the room.

Notice that in Urdu/Hindi, whether the word is yyh[3] or vwh,[1] it can mean he, she, it, or they, and it is the form of the <u>verb</u> that follows that will often tell you which it does mean.   In other words, the position is the opposite of what it is in English.   In English you often have a simple verb, with a variety of pronouns: in Urdu/Hindi you have a simple pronoun, with a variety of verbs.

English		Urdu/Hindi
		vwh[1] rəhti həy
She		rəhta həy
He	live(s)	rəhti həyŋ
They		rəhte həyŋ

In neither case is there anything unclear about the meaning.   Let me remind you again of what I said above (p.19), that this explains the difficulty South Asians find in getting their 'he' and 'she' right when speaking English.   And where the form of the verb indicates that the meaning of yyh or vwh is singular it also indicates status.   (In the case of real plurals, of course, the verb doesn't show status.)

There will be a chance to practise all these things in the units that follow.

By the end of unit 4 you already had all the Urdu/Hindi you need to say a good many things about yourself - your name, where you live, and what work you do.   Unit 5 taught you how to say many of the same things about your fathers, mothers, husbands and wives.   (You can't however talk yet about their <u>names</u>.   To do this you need a grammatical rule which you haven't yet learnt.)   You can now enlarge the range to take in daughters, sons, sisters and brothers, and it will be good practice for you to do this before you go any further.   Take care to keep within the structures you know.   Remember (i) that you must use vwh[1] for people absent, (ii) a younger brother or sister is junior to you and so you must talk of them in the singular, and (iii) an older brother or sister is senior to you and so you must talk of them in the courteous plural.

---

1.   H. plu. ve.
2.   H. stri.
3.   H. plu. ye.

For example, about a younger brother, you might say:

> mera bhai London meŋ rəhta həy.
> vwh soʃəl vərkər həy.
> vwh Ealing meŋ kam kərta həy.

But about an elder brother, you might say:

> merę bhai London meŋ rəhte həyŋ.
> vwh[1] ţicər həyŋ.
> vwh[1] Brixton meŋ kam kərte həyŋ.

Similarly, about a younger sister, you might say:

> meri bəhyn Reading meŋ rəhti həy.

> > > > etc.

But about an older sister, you would say:

> meri bəhyn London meŋ rəhti həyŋ.

> > > > etc.

---

1. H. ve.

Status and Imperatives: Summary of new material

1.   vwh[1] Oxford meŋ rəhti həyŋ.   She (absent, <u>ap</u> status) lives in Oxford.

2.   vwh[1] Oxford meŋ rəhti həyŋ.   They (absent, f.) live in Oxford.

3.   vwh[1] Oxford meŋ rəhte həyŋ.   He (absent, <u>ap</u> status) lives in Oxford.

4.   vwh[1] Oxford meŋ rəhte həyŋ.   They (absent, m. or m./f. mixed) live in Oxford.

5.   twm Oxford meŋ rəhti ho.   You (junior, f.) live in Oxford.

6.   twm Oxford meŋ rəhte ho.   You (junior, m.) live in Oxford.

7.   vwh Oxford meŋ rəhti həy.   She (absent, junior) lives in Oxford.

8.   vwh Oxford meŋ rəhta həy.   He (absent, junior) lives in Oxford.

9.   twm kəhaŋ rəhti ho?   Where do you (f. junior) live?

10.   twm kəhaŋ rəhte ho?   Where do you (m. junior) live?

Forming the imperative:

	infinitive	root	'ap' imperative = root + <u>iye</u>	'twm' imperative = root + <u>o</u>
to say	kəhna	kəh	kəhiye	kəho
to ask, enquire	puchna	puch	puchiye	pucho
to listen	swnna	swn	swniye	swno
to see, look at	dekhna	dekh	dekhiye	dekho
to tell	bətana	bəta	bətaiye	bətao
to come	ana	a	aiye	ao
to sit down	bəyʈhna	bəyʈh	bəyʈhiye	bəyʈho
to read	pərhna	pərh	pərhiye	pərho

If in doubt use the -<u>iye</u> forms!

_____

1.   H. ve.

The present tense - complete!

You can now survey <u>all</u> the present tense forms.   At this point
I should tell you that the present tense is formed by adding the

$$-\underline{ti}, \quad -\underline{ta}, \quad -\underline{te}$$

endings to the root and adding <u>huŋ, həy, həyŋ</u>, etc. as appropriate.
Grammars call this form in -<u>ti</u>, -<u>ta</u>, -<u>te</u> the present participle.

From this, working backwards, you can deduce other forms of the
verb.   If <u>rəhta</u> is the root plus -<u>ta</u> then:

the root is	<u>rəh</u>
the infinitive is	<u>rəhna</u>
the <u>ap</u> imperative is	<u>rəhiye</u>
the <u>twm</u> imperative is	<u>rəho</u>

The basic meaning of <u>rəhna</u> is 'to remain' or to 'stay'.   It is
by an extension of this basic meaning that it also means 'to live,
reside'.

Feminine forms

məyŋ rəhti huŋ	I live
[tu rəhti həy]	[thou livest]
yyh rəhti həy	she[1,2] lives
vwh rəhti həy	she[3,2] lives
həm rəhte həyŋ[4]	we live
ap rəhti həyŋ	you live
twm rəhti ho	you[2] live
yyh[5] rəhti həyŋ	they[1] live, she lives[1,7]
vwh[6] rəhti həyŋ	they[3] live, she[3,7] lives

Masculine forms *

məyŋ rəhta huŋ	I live
[tu rəhta həy]	[thou livest]
yyh rəhta həy	he[1,2] lives
vwh rəhta həy	he[3,2] lives
həm rəhte həyŋ	we live
ap rəhte həyŋ	you live
twm rəhte ho	you[2] live
yyh[5] rəhte həyŋ	they[1] live, he[1,7] lives
vwh[6] rəhte həyŋ	they[3] live, he[3,7] lives

---

1.   present.
2.   junior status.
3.   absent.
4.   H., and many Panjabi speakers, rəhti həyŋ.

5.   H. ye.
6.   H. ve.
7.   <u>ap</u> status.

---

*   The masculine plural forms are also used for mixed m. and f.
subjects.

Unit 9.   Daily routines

In this unit we're going to talk about daily routines - other people's, mine, and yours.

You'll need to know quite a few new words and phrases. The key ones are these:

sat,	aʈh,	nəw,	dəs,	gyara,	bara
7	8	9	10	11	12

(Note that to an Urdu/Hindi speaker <u>sat</u> and <u>aʈh</u> sound very different - the last sound of <u>sat</u> is an unaspirated dental: the last of <u>aʈh</u> is an aspirated retroflex.

....bəje - [at] ... o'clock

wʈhna - to rise, get up. Present tense <u>mayŋ wʈhti huŋ</u>, etc.

(You must hear clearly the aspirated retroflex followed at once by the unaspirated dental.   If it helps you to say the word better, regard the <u>wʈh</u> and the -<u>ti</u> etc. as two separate words for this purpose.)

naʃta - breakfast

naʃta kərna - 'to do breakfast', to have breakfast

I'm deliberately not giving you any other explanations at this point.

On the next page are numbered pictures illustrating the daily routine of Jamila, a Pakistani woman who works in an office.   Facing the page of pictures is a page of sentences telling you what she does at different times of day.

Listen to the sentences, reading them as you do so, and see if you can work out what each of them probably means.

I shall give you full notes and explanations after that - on a separate page!

1. <u>jəmila</u> sat bəje wʈhti həy.

2. vwh aʈh bəje naʃta kərti həy.

3. vwh naʃte meŋ ek ənɖa əwr do tos khati həy.

4. vwh nəw bəje ghər se ɳykəlti həy.

5. vwh dəs bəje dəftər pəhwŋcti həy.

6. vwh ek bəje dopəhr ka khana khati həy.

7. vwh car bəje cae piti həy.

8. vwh pəŋc bəje dəftər se ɳykəlti həy.

9. vwh aʈh bəje rat ka khana khati həy.

10. vwh dəs bəje soti həy.

Notes

naʃte meŋ	'in breakfast', for breakfast [1]
ənɖa	egg
tos	toast
khana	to eat
ghər	house, home
-se nykəlna	'to emerge from', to go out of, leave
dəftər	office
pəhwŋcna	to arrive

Notice Urdu/Hindi says 'arrives the office', not 'arrives at the office'.

dopəhr ka khana	'food of midday', lunch, midday meal

Note that khana is both a verb, 'to eat' and a noun, 'food'.

cae	tea
pina	to drink
rat ka khana	'food of night', evening meal, supper
sona	to sleep, go to bed

Now work out how to describe your own daily routine, on the pattern of Jamila's - even if this pattern doesn't exactly fit yours. (You can, of course, change the times if you like.)

Then work out the questions you'd ask Jamila about her routine to get the answers she'd give you.

e.g. ap kytne bəje wʈhti həyŋ?

When you've worked out how to describe your own daily routine it's worth while learning it by heart, so that if you're asked

ap dyn bhər meŋ kya kərti həyŋ?
What do you do in the course of the day?
(literally 'in day-full')

you can respond with a full account.

---

1. naʃta = breakfast, naʃte meŋ = 'in breakfast'. In a later unit I'll explain this change of -a to -e.

9.2 Others' daily routines

Now listen to, and read, the following dialogue:

1. A.   məyŋ aţh bəje wţhti huŋ.   ba∫ir, ap kytne bəje wţhte həyŋ?

2. B.   məyŋ sat bəje wţhta huŋ.

3. A.   ap ki bivi[1] bhi sat bəje wţhti həyŋ?

4. B.   meri bivi[1] chəy bəje wţhti həyŋ.

5. A.   ap kytne bəje na∫ta kərte həyŋ?

6. B.   məyŋ saɽhe aţh bəje na∫ta kərta huŋ.

7. A.   ap na∫te meŋ kya khate həyŋ?

8. B.   məyŋ do əņḍe əwr do tos khata huŋ.

9. A.   ap ki bivi[1] ap ke sath na∫ta kərti həyŋ?

10. B.   ji nəhiŋ.   bivi[1] nəw bəje na∫ta kərti həyŋ.

11. A.   ap ki bivi[1] na∫te meŋ kya khati həyŋ?

12. B.   bivi[1] kya khati həyŋ?   mwjhe malum nəhiŋ.   məyŋ pəwne nəw bəje ghər se nykəlta huŋ.

13. A.   ap dəftər kytne bəje pəhwŋcte həyŋ?

14. B.   məyŋ dəftər meŋ kam nəhiŋ kərtaː fəykţri meŋ kam kərta huŋ.

15. A.   əccha, fəykţri meŋ kam kərte həyŋ?   ap fəykţri kytne bəje pəhwŋcte həyŋ?

16. B.   nəw bəje pəhwŋcta huŋ.   fəykţri mere ghər ke pas həy.

17. A.   ap ki bivi[1] bhi fəykţri meŋ kam kərti həyŋ?

18. B.   ji nəhiŋ, vwh ghər ke bahər kam nəhiŋ kərtiŋ.

19. A.   əwr ap ka beţa?   vwh fəykţri meŋ kam kərta həy?

20. B.   ji nəhiŋ, vwh berozgar[2] həy.

21. A.   əwr ap ki bəhu?

22. B.   vwh ghər meŋ kam kərti həy.   do choţe bəcce həyŋ; wn ki dekh-bhal kərti həy.

---

1. H. pətni.
2. H. (and Urdu) bekar.

23. A. ap dopəhr ka khana kəhaŋ khate həyŋ?   fəykʈri meŋ
        khana khate həyŋ?

24. B. ji haŋ, fəykʈri meŋ kəynʈin həy.

25. A. əwr car bəje cae pite həyŋ?

26. B. ji haŋ.

27. A. ap fəykʈri se kytne bəje nykəlte həyŋ?

28. B. məyŋ fəykʈri se paŋc bəje nykəlta huŋ.

29. A. Sue, ap ʈicər həyŋ, na?

30. S. ji haŋ, ʈicər huŋ.

31. A. ap kytne bəje skul se nykəlti həyŋ?   əwr kytne bəje
        ghər vapəs pəhwŋcti həyŋ?

32. S. məyŋ saʈhe car bəje skul se nykəlti huŋ əwr səva paŋc
        bəje ghər vapəs pəhwŋcti huŋ.   mera ghər skul se kafi
        dur həy - aʈh mil dur.

33. A. əccha, ap kytne bəje rat ka khana khati həyŋ?

34. S. kəbhi pəwne aʈh bəje, kəbhi aʈh bəje, kəbhi səva aʈh
        bəje, kəbhi saʈhe aʈh bəje!   kwch təy nəhiŋ!

35. A. əwr ap kytne bəje soti həyŋ?

36. S. gyara, səva gyara bəje.   əb bətaiye, məyŋ kytne bəje
        wʈhti huŋ?

37. A. pəwne aʈh bəje?   aʈh bəje?

38. S. ji haŋ, pəwne aʈh bəje, aʈh bəje.

Notes

In these sentences you hear the words for quarter to, quarter past, and half past

pəwne aʈh bəje	at a quarter to eight
səva aʈh bəje	at a quarter past eight
saɽhe aʈh bəje	at half past eight

9.   -ke sath - with-

10. and 12.   People will quite commonly refer to their wives as simply 'bivi'[1] rather than 'meri bivi'.[1]

19.   -ke bahər - outside-

20.   A's use of the singular would imply that B's son is probably young enough to be her son.

22.   behu - son's wife, daughter-in-law.   She will commonly live with her husband in his parents' home.

25.   -ki dekh-bhal kərna - 'to do the looking-after of', to look after.

32.   ap ʈicər həyŋ, na? - You're a teacher, aren't you?

skul   Native speakers of Urdu often pronounce it yskul, while Panjabis say səkul.   But the pronunciation skul is becoming increasingly common.

34.   ghər vapəs pəhwŋcna - to arrive back home.

37.   kəbhi..., kəbhi... - Sometimes...., sometimes

kwch - some, something, anything

kwch təy nəhiŋ - 'anything fixed not' - nothing fixed

English translation of sentences 1-38

1.   A.   I get up at 8 o'clock.   Bashir, what time do you get up?

2.   B.   I get up at 7o'clock.

3.   A.   Does your wife also get up at 7 o'clock?

---

1.   H. pətni.

4. B. My wife gets up at 6 o'clock.

5. A. What time do you have breakfast?

6. B. I have breakfast at half-past 8.

7. A. What do you have for breakfast? ('What do you eat in breakfast?')

8. B. I eat two eggs and two pieces of toast.

9. A. Does your wife have breakfast with you?

10. B. No, my wife has breakfast at 9 o'clock.

11. A. What does your wife have for breakfast?

12. B. What does my wife have? I don't know. I leave the house at a quarter to nine.

13. A. What time do you get to the office?

14. B. I don't work in an office. I work in a factory.

15. A. Oh? You work in a factory? What time do you get to the factory?

16. B. I get there at 9. The factory is near my house.

17. A. Does your wife too work in a factory?

18. B. No, she doesn't work outside the home.

19. A. And your son? Does he work in a factory?

20. B. No. He's unemployed.

21. A. And your daughter-in-law?

22. B. She works at home. [There] are two small children. She looks after them.

23. A. Where do you have lunch ('eat your midday meal')? Do you have it in the factory?

24. B. Yes. There's a canteen in the factory.

25. A. And at 4 o'clock do you have tea?

26. B. Yes.

27. A. What time do you leave the factory?

28. B. I leave the factory at 5 o'clock.

29. A. Sue, you're a teacher, aren't you?

30. S. Yes, I'm a teacher.

31. A. What time do you leave the school? And what time do you get back home?

32. S. I leave the school at half past four and get back home at a quarter past five. My house is quite a long way from the school - eight miles.

33. A. I see. What time do you have your evening meal?

34. S. Sometimes at a quarter to eight, sometimes at eight, sometimes at a quarter past eight, sometimes at half past eight! Nothing fixed!

35. A. And what time do you go to bed?

36. S. Eleven or a quarter past. Now [you] tell me. What time do I get up?

37. A. A quarter to eight? Eight o'clock.

38. S. Yes, a quarter to eight or eight o'clock.

Obviously you can model innumerable sentences on these, using the whole range of forms you have now learnt, using, as appropriate

məyŋ	naʃta	kərti huŋ	/	nəhiŋ kərti
		kərta	/	kərta
ap		kərti həyŋ	/	kərtiŋ
		kərte	/	kərte
twm		kərti ho	/	kərtiŋ
		kərte	/	kərte
yyh[1]		kərti həyŋ	/	kərtiŋ
		kərte	/	kərte
vwh[2]		kərti həyŋ	/	kərtiŋ
		kərte	/	kərte
yyh		kərti həy	/	kərti
		kərta	/	kərta
vwh		kərti həy	/	kərti
		kərta	/	kərta

Pick sentences at random and practice doing this.

---

1. H. ye.
2. H. ve.

To follow unit 9

(All the questions are put to a woman.)

1.	Q.	ap kytne bəje wʈhti həyŋ?
2.	W.	məyŋ .... bəje wʈhti huŋ.
3.	Q.	ap kytne bəje naʃta kərti həyŋ?
4.	W.	məyŋ .... bəje naʃta kərti huŋ.
5.	Q.	ap naʃte meŋ kya khati həyŋ?
6.	W.	məyŋ naʃte meŋ .... khati huŋ.
7.	Q.	ap ghər se kytne bəje nykəlti həyŋ?
8.	W.	məyŋ ghər se .... bəje nykəlti huŋ.
9.	Q.	ap kytne bəje ⌈dəftər, skul ...⌋ pəhwŋcti həyŋ?
10.	W.	məyŋ .... bəje .... pəhwŋcti huŋ.
11.	Q.	ap dopəhr ka khana kytne bəje khati həyŋ?
12.	W.	məyŋ dopəhr ka khana .... bəje khati huŋ.
13.	Q.	ap kytne bəje cae piti həyŋ?
14.	W.	məyŋ .... bəje cae piti huŋ.
15.	Q.	ap kytne bəje .... se nykəlti həyŋ?
16.	W.	məyŋ .... bəje .... se nykəlti huŋ.
17.	Q.	ap ghər vapəs kytne bəje pəhwŋcti həyŋ?
18.	W.	məyŋ ghər vapəs .... bəje pəhwŋcti huŋ.
19.	Q.	ap kytne bəje rat ka khana khati həyŋ?
20.	W.	məyŋ .... bəje rat ka khana khati huŋ.
21.	Q.	ap kytne bəje soti həyŋ?
22.	W.	məyŋ .... bəje soti huŋ.

The same questions can be put to M.   In that case the verb in the question will be

-te həyŋ?

and in the answer

-ta huŋ

You can also practise asking the same questions, as appropriate, about

ap ke ʃəwhər[1]
ap ki bivi[2]
ap ke valyd[3]
ap ki valyda[4]
ap ke beʈe
ap ki beʈi

You should find all or most of the models you need for appropriate answers in sentences 1-38 of unit 9.

---

1.   H. pəti.
2.   H. pətni.
3.   H. pytaji.
4.   H. mata ji.

English translation of sentences 1-14

1. A. Brian, you live in Oxford, don't you?

2. B. Yes, I live in Oxford.

3. A. Have you always lived in Oxford?

4. B. No, I haven't always lived in Oxford.

5. A. How many years have you lived in Oxford?

6. B. I've lived in Oxford for twelve years.

7. A. Where did you live before that?

8. B. Before that I used to live in Liverpool.

9. A. I see, Kate, you too live in Oxford, don't you?

10. K. Yes, I too live in Oxford.

11. A. Have you always lived in Oxford?

12. K. No, I've lived in Oxford six years.

13. A. Six years?   Where did you live before that?

14. K. Before that I used to live in Banbury.

Notes

rəhe həyŋ, rəha huŋ, rəhi həyŋ, rəhi huŋ are forms of a tense you haven't met before.   You'll have guessed that they mean 'have lived'.   The whole tense conforms exactly to the pattern of the present tense, 'rəhta huŋ'.   In other words, if you drop the 't' from the present tense forms you get this tense.

You know that 'məyŋ rəhta huŋ', 'ap rəhte həyŋ', etc. mean 'I live', 'you live' and so on.   Note that Urdu/Hindi idiom differs from English.   In English you say (e.g.)

I have lived in Oxford for six years

while in Urdu/Hindi you say the equivalent of

I live in Oxford since six years

rəhta tha is the corresponding past tense to the present rəhta huŋ and the -a changes to -e, -i, etc. in exactly the same way.   It means 'used to live'.

10.2   Where were you born?   Where have you lived since then?

Now listen to, and read, the next dialogue.   These are new words you will meet

məyŋ pəyda hua tha / pəyda hui thi means 'I was born'.

Note that the pəyda never changes its form, but that the hua tha, hui thi, hue the, hui thiŋ change on the usual pattern.

sal means 'year' or 'years'

vəhaŋ means 'there'

rəha, rəhi, rəhe, rəhiŋ mean 'lived'

ws ke bad means 'after that'

Banbury ke bad means 'after Banbury'

gəya, gəi, gəe, gəiŋ mean 'went'

aya, ai, ae, aiŋ mean 'came'

pəhle means 'ago'

kytne sal pəhle? means 'How many years ago?'

15. A.   məyŋ <u>ləndən</u> meŋ pəyda hui thi. <u>Ken</u>, ap kəhaŋ pəyda
          hue the?

16. K.   məyŋ <u>Chester</u> meŋ pəyda hua tha.

17. A.   əwr <u>Sue</u>? ap? ap kəhaŋ pəyda hui thiŋ?

18. S.   məyŋ <u>Reading</u> meŋ pəyda hui thi.

19. A.   əccha, swniye. məyŋ <u>ləndən</u> meŋ pəyda hui thi əwr bara
          sal vəhaŋ rəhi. <u>Ken</u>, ap <u>Chester</u> meŋ pəyda hue the.
          ap kytne sal vəhaŋ rəhe?

20. K.   məyŋ pəŋc sal vəhaŋ rəha.

21. A.   swniye. məyŋ <u>ləndən</u> meŋ pəyda hui thi əwr bara sal vəhaŋ
          rəhi. ws ke bad məyŋ <u>Banbury</u> gəi, əwr vəhaŋ chəy sal
          rəhi. <u>John</u>, ap bətaiye...

22. J.   məyŋ <u>Sheffield</u> meŋ pəyda hua tha. məyŋ pəŋc sal vəhaŋ
          rəha. ws ke bad məyŋ <u>Leeds</u> gəya, əwr gyara sal vəhaŋ
          rəha.

23. A.   ʃabaʃ! bəhwt əccha. əb <u>Carol</u>, ap kəhiye.

24. C.   məyŋ <u>Cambridge</u> meŋ pəyda hui thi. məyŋ aṭh sal vəhaŋ rəhi.
          ws ke bad məyŋ <u>Harlow</u> gəi. məyŋ sat sal vəhaŋ rəhi.

25. A.   ʃabaʃ! bəhwt əccha. əb swniye: <u>Banbury</u> ke bad məyŋ <u>Oxford</u>
          ai - <u>Oxford ai</u>. məyŋ chəy sal se <u>Oxford</u> meŋ rəhti huŋ.
          <u>Brian</u>, ap <u>Oxford</u> meŋ rəhte həyŋ, na?

26. B.   ji haŋ, məyŋ <u>Oxford</u> meŋ rəhta huŋ.

27. A.   ap həmeʃa <u>Oxford</u> meŋ nəhiŋ rəhe həyŋ. ap <u>Oxford</u> kytne
          sal pəhle ae? <u>Oxford</u> meŋ kytne sal se rəhte həyŋ?

28. B.   məyŋ <u>Oxford</u> bara sal pəhle aya. <u>Oxford</u> meŋ bara sal se
          rəhta huŋ.

English translation of sentences 15-28

15. A.   I was born in London.   Ken, where were you born?

16. K.   I was born in Chester.

17. A.   And Sue?   You?   Where were you born?

18. S.   I was born in Reading.

19. A.   Alright, listen.   I was born in London and lived there
         twelve years.   Ken, you were born in Chester.   How many
         years did you live there?

20. K.   I lived there five years.

21. A.   Listen.   I was born in London and lived there twelve years.
         After that I went to Banbury, and lived there six years.
         John, you tell us...

22. J.   I was born in Sheffield.   I lived there five years.   After
         that I went to Leeds, and lived there eleven years.

23. A.   Well done!   Very good.   Now Carol, you say...

24. C.   I was born in Cambridge.   I lived there eight years.   After
         that I went to Harlow.   I lived there seven years.

25. A.   Well done!   Very good.   Now listen: After Banbury I came
         to Oxford - came to Oxford.   I've lived in Oxford for six
         years.   Brian, you live in Oxford, don't you?

26. B.   Yes.   I live in Oxford.

27. A.   You haven't always lived in Oxford.   How many years ago did
         you come to Oxford?   How many years have you lived in
         Oxford?

28. B.   I came to Oxford twelve years ago.   I've lived in Oxford
         twelve years.

Notes

21. Banbury gəi.   Note that here there is nothing corresponding to
English 'to' - cf. unit 9, sentence 5.   So also 'Oxford ai' in 25.)

In this dialogue you meet the simple past tense

        I lived   məyŋ rəha/rəhi
        I went   məyŋ gəya/gəi
        I came   məyŋ aya/ai

In the preceding dialogue you met the form

I have lived   məyŋ rəha huŋ/rəhi huŋ[1]

So

      I have gone would be   məyŋ gəya huŋ/gəi huŋ

      I have come would be   məyŋ aya huŋ/ai huŋ

In unit 8 you were told that

The infinitive ends in -na

rəhna	to live, to remain
kəhna	to say
swnna	to hear

The root is the infinitive minus its -na ending

rəh

kəh

swn

The present participle is root + -ta, -ti, -te, etc.

rəhta, rəhti, rəhte   etc.

kəhta, kəhti, kəhte,   etc.

swnta, swnti, swnte,   etc.

Two tenses are formed from this:

məyŋ rəhti huŋ	I live
məyŋ rəhti thi	I used to live
məyŋ kəhti huŋ	I say
məyŋ kəhti thi	I used to say

Now you can add that

The past participle is root + -a, -i, -e, etc.

rəha, rəhi, rəhe

kəha, kəhi, kəhe

swna, swni, swne

---

1.   but remember that 'I have lived in London for twelve years' is, in Urdu/Hindi usage, 'I live in London since twelve years'.

Several tenses are formed from the past participle, of which you've now met two

<u>məyŋ rəha/rəhi</u>	I lived
<u>məyŋ rəha huŋ/rəhi huŋ</u>	I have lived
<u>məyŋ gəya/gəi</u>	I went
<u>məyŋ gəya huŋ/gəi huŋ</u>	I have gone
<u>məyŋ aya/ai</u>	I came
<u>məyŋ aya huŋ/ai huŋ</u>	I have come

Some (not many!) past participles don't follow the regular rules. Thus roots that end in a vowel, for obvious reasons, stick in a <u>y</u> before the -<u>a</u> ending, e.g.

<u>ana</u> - to come

root <u>a</u>

past participle not 'a-a' (which isn't felt to be easy to say)

but <u>aya</u>

(However, since there's no difficulty in saying

<u>ae</u>, <u>ai</u>

the <u>y</u> isn't usually inserted in these forms.)[1]

And <u>jana</u>, to go (like English 'to go') has an irregular past.

The past participle is not 'ja-ya', but

<u>gəya, gəe, gəi</u>

10.3 <u>Who's been where</u>?

Now listen to, and read, the next dialogue. It doesn't introduce many new words or forms, and you will be able to make a reasonable guess at most of them. So first, just listen and read, and get the general sense without pausing to look up the words you don't know. You may find it helpful to read again the sentences in unit 4 and sentences 20-23 in unit 5 before you tackle this dialogue.

Then use the notes at the end, and listen and read again to get the <u>full</u> meaning.

---

1. in Hindi spelling, it <u>is</u> inserted.

29. A. Ian, ap bətaiye, ap kəyaŋ pəyda hue the? vəɣəyra
vəɣəyra... ap səmjhe?

30. I. ji nəhiŋ, məyŋ nəhiŋ səmjha.

31. A. əccha; kəhiye, 'məyŋ ləndən meŋ pəyda hua tha əwr do sal
vəhaŋ rəha. ws ke bad... 'vəɣəyra vəɣəyra. əb səmjhe?

32. I. ji haŋ, əb səmjha. məyŋ ləndən meŋ pəyda hua tha. meri bəhyn
Sarah bhi ləndən meŋ pəyda hui thi. məyŋ pəŋc sal vəhaŋ rəha.
ws ke bad mere valydəyn[1] Crawley gəe.

33. A. Crawley kəhaŋ həy?

34. I. Crawley Sussex meŋ həy. nəya ʃəhr həy. Crawley meŋ
həm tin sal rəhe. ws ke bad həm Harlow gəe.

35. A. Harlow? Harlow kəhaŋ həy?

36. I. Harlow Essex meŋ həy, ləndən se bis pəccis mil dur. yyh
bhi nəya ʃəhr həy. həm Harlow meŋ tera sal rəhe, əwr ws
ke bad jənubi[2] ləndən ae. məyŋ syrf tin sal Harlow meŋ
rəha. ws ke bad məyŋ Sussex yunivərsyʈi gəya, əwr Brighton
meŋ pəŋc sal rəha. ws ke bad məyŋ hyndostan - bharət -
gəya.

37. A. əccha, ap bharət gəe həyŋ? vəhaŋ rəhe bhi həyŋ?

38. I. ji haŋ, do dəfa gəya huŋ. pakystan bhi ek dəfa gəya
huŋ. pəhli dəfa ek sal rəha, əwr dusri dəfa chəy məhine.
dusri dəfa məyŋ pakystan bhi gəya əwr kwch dyn ek gaoŋ
kənyal meŋ rəha.

39. A. gaoŋ meŋ kytne dyn rəhe?

40. I. mwjhe yad nəhiŋ. təqribən[3] do həfte.

41. A. kənyal kəhaŋ həy?

42. I. kənyal pənjab meŋ həy, jəhlwm ke qərib. pakystan ke bad
məyŋ jənubi[2] ləndən vapəs aya. vəhaŋ gyara sal se rəhta huŋ.
vəhaŋ kam bhi kərta huŋ. məyŋ ʈicər huŋ. mera skul
plumstead meŋ həy, ghər se sat mil dur.

43. A. ap ke valyd,[4] mwjhe malum həy, bəhwt dəfa bharət əwr[5]
pakystan gəe həyŋ, əwr rəhe bhi həyŋ. ap ki valyda[5] kəbhi
gəi həyŋ?

---

1. H. mata pyta.
2. H. dəkʃyni.
3. H. or, ləg bhəg.
4. H. pyta ji.
5. H. mata ji.

44. I.   ji haŋ, kəi dəfa.   car dəfa gəi həyŋ.   meri bəhyneŋ
         (meri do bəhyneŋ həyŋ) kəbhi nəhiŋ gəiŋ.

45. A.   Sue, ap Reading meŋ kytne sal se rəhti həyŋ?

46. S.   məyŋ tin sal se Reading meŋ rəhti huŋ.₂ ws se pəhle məyŋ
         əwr meri valyda¹ Slough meŋ rəhte the.² məyŋ tin sal pəhle
         Reading ai.   əb valyda¹ bhi ai həyŋ - tin məhine pəhle aiŋ.

Notes on sentences 29-46

29. vəɣəyra vəɣəyra - 'etcetera, etcetera' - Urdu/Hindi speakers
usually repeat the word rather than just saying it once.   Note the ɣ
sound - you met it before in motəɣərbi, one of the villages mentioned
in unit 4.

     ap səmjhe? - 'do you understand?' (Literally, 'Did you understand?' -
because Urdu/Hindi idiom uses the past whsre English uses the present.)

     Quite commonly the order is inverted, and people will ask səmjhe ap? -
or even simply səmjhe?

     A woman would be asked ap səmjhiŋ, or səmjhiŋ ap? or simply səmjhiŋ?
(Note that the 'h' must be clearly heard when you say these words.)

32. thi (in line 2).   So is Sarah his elder or his younger sister?

34. nəya (f. nəi, m. plu. nəe) - new.

36. bis pəccis - 'twenty twenty-five' - i.e., twenty to twenty-five.

     syrf - only.

     hyndostan - India.   But bharət is increasingly common.   See the
last note on p.40.

     yndiya is also commonly used.

37. Note the position of the bhi.

38. dəfa - time.   do dəfa - 'two time', twice.

     pəhli dəfa - the first time

     dusri dəfa - the second time

39. məhina - month

     kwch - some

     dyn - day, days

----

1. H. mata ji.
2. H., and in the Urdu of many Panjabis, rəhti thiŋ.

ek gaoŋ kənyal – a village called Kanyal.

40. təqribən[1] – approximately, about.

Notice the q sound. You met it before in Unit 4, sentence 12.

vapəs aya – come back.

42. Again note the position of the bhi.

43. kəbhi – ever.

44. kəi – several. See note on Unit 4, sentence 16.

kəbhi nəhiŋ – never ('ever not').

In these sentences you have encountered some numbers – 20 and 25 – that you hadn't met before. Counting in Urdu/Hindi isn't as simple as it is in English, as this example illustrates.

For everyday purposes you need only to be able to count up to 31 (so that you know how to tell the exact time, and the dates – and we shall be dealing with this in a later unit) and these numbers are given in appendix 3. (Any others you may need on particular occasions you can ask ad hoc.) In everyday conversation it is easy enough to say (as in sentence 34 above) 'bis pəccis' – 20 to 25 – instead of the exact number. (Harlow is in fact 23 – teis – miles from London.)

For a full account of the numbers, and how to learn and to use them, see Part II.

You may also like to know at this point a little more about how to express times, periods of time, and so on.

You have had sentences from which you can deduce that

ek dyn	=	one day	and	kəi dyn	=	several days
ek həfta	=	one week		kəi həfte	=	several weeks
ek məhina	=	one month		kəi məhine	=	several months
ek sal	=	one year		kəi sal	=	several years

---

1. H. or, ləg bhəg.

You have also met <u>təqribən,</u>[1]   meaning 'approximately' - and
      <u>ws se pəhle</u>   'before that'
      <u>ws ke bad</u>   'after that'

you may remember from unit 4, sentence 38 that <u>koi</u> can be used in the
same sense

<u>təqribən</u>[1] bara dyn	about 12 days
<u>koi bara dyn</u>	some 12 days
<u>dəs bara dyn</u>	'ten twelve days'

are all virtually interchangeable.

If you want to say 'a little before that' you can say '<u>ws se zəra</u>
<u>pəhle</u>' and 'a little after that' is <u>ws ke zəra bad</u>, with the <u>zəra</u>,
meaning 'a little' sandwiched between the <u>se</u> and the <u>pəhle</u> and the <u>ke</u>
and the <u>bad</u>.

You may or may not have noticed that here and there the order
of the words in a sentence may vary somewhat.   Thus

<u>məyŋ pəɲc sal vəhaŋ rəha</u>

           or

<u>məyŋ vəhaŋ pəɲc sal rəha</u>

are equally acceptable.

Similarly in other sentences, e.g. the position of <u>həmeʃa</u> in the
sentence may vary not only from speaker to speaker but also between
different utterances of one and the same speaker.

The tenses

Urdu/Hindi is more logical and consistent in its use of tenses
than English is.

Thus <u>məyŋ rəhta huŋ</u> - I live - describes an ongoing, general
process, and doesn't express the idea of something which is actually
happening at this very moment.

<u>məyŋ rəhta tha</u> - I used to live - is the corresponding <u>past</u>
tense.

<u>məyŋ rəha</u>, <u>məyŋ gəya</u> correspond to I lived, I went.

<u>məyŋ rəha huŋ</u>, <u>məyŋ gəya huŋ</u> correspond to I have lived, I have
gone.

---

1.   H. or, ləg bhəg.

But in English 'I lived' is also often used in exactly the same sense as 'I used to live'.   You can say

>   Before that I lived in Croydon

>   or

>   Before that I used to live in Croydon

and both mean the same.

In Urdu/Hindi, when 'I lived' = 'I used to live', you must use

>   mayŋ rəhta tha

Or, to put it in another way, where you could only say 'I lived' in English, you say mayŋ rəha in Urdu/Hindi, and where you could say 'I used to live' in English, you must say mayŋ rəhta tha in Urdu/Hindi.

Thus:

>   Before that I lived in London

>   or

>   Before that I used to live in London

will be:

>   ws se pəhle mayŋ ləndən meŋ rəhta tha

But

>   I lived there five years

will be:

>   mayŋ vəhaŋ panc sal rəha

because you couldn't say in English 'I used to live there five years' - only 'I lived there five years'.

Table of present and past tenses covered so far

I live

Feminine forms

məyŋ rəhti huŋ	I live
[tu rəhti həy]	[thou livest]
yyh rəhti həy	she[1,2] lives
vwh rəhti həy	she[3,2] lives
həm rəhte həyŋ[4]	we live
ap rəhti həyŋ	you live
twm rəhti ho	you[2] live
yyh[5] rəhti həyŋ	they[1] live she[1,7] lives
vwh[6] rəhti həyŋ	they[3] live, she[3,7] lives

Masculine forms*

məyŋ rəhta huŋ	I live
[tu rəhta həy]	[thou livest]
yyh rəhta həy	he[1,2] lives
vwh rəhta həy	he[3,2] lives
həm rəhte həyŋ	we live
ap rəhte həyŋ	you live
twm rəhte ho	you[2] live
yyh[5] rəhte həyŋ	they[1] live he[1,7] lives
vwh[6] rəhte həyŋ	they[3] live he[3,7] lives

I used to live

Feminine forms

məyŋ rəhti thi	I used to live
[tu rəhti thi]	[thou used to live]
yyh rəhti thi	she[1,2] used to live
vwh rəhti thi	she[3,2] used to live
həm rəhte the[8]	we used to live
ap rəhti thiŋ	you used to live
twm rəhti thiŋ	you[2] used to live
yyh[5] rəhti thiŋ	they[1] used to live she[1,7] used to live
vwh[6] rəhti thiŋ	they[3] used to live she[3,7] used to live

Masculine forms*

məyŋ rəhta tha	I used to live
[tu rəhta tha]	[thou used to live]
yyh rəhta tha	he[1,2] used to live
vwh rəhta tha	he[3,2] used to live
həm rəhte the	we used to live
ap rəhte the	you used to live
twm rəhte the	you[2] used to live
yyh[5] rəhte the	they[1] used to live he[1,7] used to live
vwh[6] rəhte the	they[3] used to live he[3,7] used to live

---

1. present.
2. junior status.
3. absent.
4. H., and many Panjabi speakers; rəhti həyŋ.
5. H. ye.
6. H. ve.
7. ap status.
8. H., and many Panjabi speakers, rəhti thiŋ.

---

* The masculine plural forms are also used for mixed m. and f. subjects.

I lived

Feminine forms

məyŋ rəhi	I lived
[tu rəhi]	[thou livedst]
yyh rəhi	she[1,2] lived
vwh rəhi	she[3,2] lived
həm rəhe[4]	we lived
ap rəhiŋ	you lived
twm rəhiŋ	you[2] lived
yyh[5] rəhiŋ	they[1] lived, she[1,7] lived
vwh[6] rəhiŋ	they[3] lived she[3,7] lived

Masculine forms *

məyŋ rəha	I lived
[tu rəha]	[thou livedst]
yyh rəha	he[1,2] lived
vwh rəha	he[3,2] lived
həm rəhe	we lived
ap rəhe	you lived
twm rəhe	you[2] lived
yyh[5] rəhe	they[1] lived, he[1,7] lived
vwh[6] rəhe	they[3] lived, he[3,7] lived

I have lived

Feminine forms

məyŋ rəhi huŋ	I have lived
[tu rəhi həy]	[thou hast lived]
yyh rəhi həy	she[1,2] has lived
vwh rəhi həy	she[3,2] has lived
həm rəhe həyŋ[8]	we have lived
ap rəhi həyŋ	you have lived
twm rəhi ho	you[2] have lived
yyh[5] rəhi həyŋ	they[1] have lived she[1,7] has lived
vwh[6] rəhi həyŋ	they[3] have lived she[3,7] has lived

Mascline forms *

məyŋ rəha huŋ	I have lived
[tu rəha həy]	[thou hast lived]
yyh rəha həy	he[1,2] has lived
vwh rəha həy	he[3,2] has lived
həm rəhe həyŋ	we have lived
ap rəhe həyŋ	you have lived
twm rəhe ho	you[2] have lived
yyh[5] rəhe həyŋ	they[1] have lived he[1,7] has lived
vwh[6] rəhe həyŋ	they[3] have lived he[3,7] have lived

---

1. present.
2. junior status.
3. absent.
4. H., and many Panjabi speakers; rəhiŋ.
5. H. ye.
6. H. ve.
7. ap status.
8. H., and many Panjabi speakers; rəhi həyŋ.

---

* The masculine plural forms are also used for mixed m. and f. subjects.

Note that in the tenses 'I live' and 'I have lived', where the last word is hun, hey, ho, heyn etc. you can, and often do, omit it when the statement is a negative.

I don't live in Oxford   meyn Oxford men nehin rehti hun

or

meyn Oxford men nehin rehti

I haven't lived there   meyn vehan nehin rehi hun

or

meyn vehan nehin rehi

But remember that when you omit the ho or heyn after a feminine plural you must show that it is a plural by changing rehti to rehtin

twm vehan nehin rehti ho

or

twm vehan nehin rehtin

and, similarly

twm vehan nehin rehi ho

or

twm vehan nehin rehin

Clearly, the nehin rehin form could mean equally

haven't lived

and

didn't live

Only the context will tell you which it is.

To follow unit 10

(The questions are addressed to a woman)

1. Q.   (to W.1) ap kəhaŋ rəhti həyŋ?

2. W.1   məyŋ .... meŋ rəhti huŋ.

3. Q.   ap həmeʃa ... meŋ rəhi həyŋ?

4. W.1   ji haŋ, məyŋ həmeʃa .... meŋ rəhi huŋ.

5. Q.   (to W.2) əwr ap?   ap kəhaŋ rəhti həyŋ?

6. W.2   məyŋ .... meŋ rəhti huŋ.

7. Q.   ap .... meŋ həmeʃa rəhi həyŋ?

8. W.2   ji nəhiŋ, məyŋ .... meŋ həmeʃa nəhiŋ rəhi huŋ.   məyŋ ....
          meŋ .... sal se rəhti huŋ.

9. Q.   ws se pəhle ap kəhaŋ rəhti thiŋ?

10. W.2   ws se pəhle məyŋ .... meŋ rəhti thi.

11. Q.   ap .... meŋ kytne sal rəhiŋ?

12. W.2   məyŋ .... meŋ .... sal rəhi.

To practice the same questions with M change the verbs in the
questions to

                    rəhte həyŋ
                        and
                    rəhe həyŋ

The answers will have the verb forms:

                    rəhta huŋ
                        and
                    rəha huŋ

Questions about a 3rd person (W) will have the verb forms

                    rəhti həyŋ
                        and
                    rəhi həyŋ

e.g. yyh[1] .... sal se .... meŋ rəhti həyŋ?

yyh[1] həmeʃa .... meŋ rəhi həyŋ?

Answers too will have the same verb forms.

Questions about a 3rd person (M) will have the verb forms

rəhte həyŋ

and

rəhe həyŋ

and answers too will have the same forms.

Now sentences 13-20, in all of which the questions are addressed to M.

13. Q.   ap kəhaŋ pəyda hue the?

14. M.   məyŋ .... meŋ pəyda hua tha.

15. Q.   ap kytne sal vəhaŋ rəhe?

16. M.   məyŋ .... sal vəhaŋ rəha.

17. Q.   ws ke bad ap kəhaŋ gəe?

18. M.   ws ke bad məyŋ .... gəya.   .... sal vəhaŋ rəha.

19. Q.   ws ke bad ap .... ae?

20. M.   ji haŋ, ws ke bad məyŋ .... aya.

Questions put to W would have the verb forms

pəyda hui thiŋ?
rəhiŋ?
gəiŋ?
aiŋ?

Her answers would have the forms

pəyda hui thi
rəhi
gəi
ai

___

1. H. ye.

Questions <u>about</u> W would have the same forms as questions put
<u>to</u> W - and the answers would have the same forms as the questions.

Questions about M would, similarly, have the same forms as
questions put <u>to</u> M - and the answers would have the same forms as
the questions.

If you want to attempt a more ambitious exchange than these,
model one on the patterns you will find in sentences 29-46 in unit
10.

anənd   mohən   kəmla
7   12

Unit 11.   People's names and ages

11.1 Listen to, and read, these sentences, and look at the picture
opposite.   The first six sentences are ones you've met before.   The
ones after that introduce a new pattern, but you'll probably guess
what they mean if I tell you that

wmər means 'age'

One other point: in earlier units where you've had pictures
to look at I've used yyh and yn ka/yn ki/yn ke - the form referring to
people who are present, regarding them as, so to speak, being present
in the picture.   Now I'm going to use the forms vwh, and the
possessives corresponding to it, wn ka, wn ki, wn ke, regarding them
as absent and not looking upon them as present just because we're
looking at pictures of them.

1.   vwh[1] kəmla həyŋ.

2.   wn ke do ləɾke həyŋ.

3.   vwh mohən həy.

4.   mohən wn ka bəɾa ləɾka həy.

5.   vwh anənd həy.

6.   anənd wn ka choţa ləɾka həy.

7.   bəɾe ləɾke ka nam mohən həy.

8.   choţe ləɾke ka nam anənd həy.

9.   bəɾe ləɾke ki wmər bara sal həy.

10.   choţe ləɾke ki wmər sat sal həy.

In earlier units you've learnt ap ka, ap ki, ap ke and yn ka,
yn ki, yn ke, as single units, written as two words but regarded as
one.   You'll probably have realised by now that ka, ki, ke is in fact
a postposition (meaning 'of'), like -se, -meŋ, -ke pas, -ke qərib and
so on.

---

1.   H. ve.

The sentences you have just heard show you what postpositions
do to the adjectives and nouns which precede them, or, more precisely,
what they do if these nouns belong to the class of masculine
singular nouns that end in -a.   (You'll learn later what they do
to other nouns.)   In the case of this class of nouns they change
the -a ending to -e, and this change is made in both the adjective
and the noun.   In this course we distinguish between the form
choṭa ləṛka in a sentence like

> anənd wn ka choṭa ləṛka həy

and the form choṭe ləṛke in a sentence like

> choṭe ləṛke ka nam anənd həy

by calling choṭa ləṛka the direct form.

and   choṭe ləṛke the oblique form.

So -ka, -ki, -ke is both a postposition and (as you already know)
an adjective.   In

> choṭe ləṛke ka nam

you have ka as postposition putting the preceding adjective and noun
into the oblique - and it is ka (not ki or ke) because it agrees with
nam, which is masculine singular.

And in

> choṭe ləṛke ki wmər

ki as postposition again puts the preceding adjective and noun into
the oblique - and it is ki (not ka or ke) because it agrees with
wmər, which is feminine.

Note that you have to say in Urdu/Hindi 'anənd's age is seven years'.
You can't say 'anənd is seven'.

Now let's see what happens to other classes of nouns.

```
semina        əli        fərida
  11                       9
```

11.2   Look at the picture of Ali and his daughters, and listen to, and read, these sentences:

11.   vwh[1] əli həyŋ.

12.   wn ki do ləɽkiyaŋ həyŋ.

13.   vwh səmina həy.

14.   səmina wn ki bəɽi ləɽki həy.

15.   vwh fərida həy.

16.   fərida wn ki choʈi ləɽki həy.

17.   bəɽi ləɽki ka nam səmina həy.

18.   choʈi ləɽki ka nam fərida həy.

19.   bəɽi ləɽki ki wmər gyara sal həy.

20.   choʈi ləɽki ki wmər nəw sal həy.

When you're speaking these sentences make sure that your pronunciation of 'ki choʈi ləɽki' is correct;   otherwise it won't be clear whether you're talking about a girl or a boy.   The distinction in sound between i and e, as you will have realised by now, is very often essential in making sense of what you are saying and hearing. You might feel that you're exaggerating the distinction, and making exaggerated movements of your mouth, in order to speak and be heard clearly, but there's no harm in this at all!

You'll have noticed that the adjective and noun before ki and ka don't change.   In other words the direct and the oblique forms are the same.

The same is true of the other class of feminine noun - the class that doesn't end in -i.

> meri choʈi bəhyn Sheffield meŋ rəhti həy
>
> and
>
> meri choʈi bəhyn ka nam Sally həy

---

1.   H. ve.

kəmla   gopal   rəvi
            30   18

11.3   But now look at the picture of Kamla and her two brothers, and listen to, and read, these sentences:

21.   vwh[1] kəmla ke choṭe bhai həyŋ.

22.   kəmla ke choṭe bhai ka nam rəvi həy.

23.   vwh[1] kəmla ke bəɽe bhai həyŋ.

24.   kəmla ke bəɽe bhai ka nam gopal həy.

25.   kəmla ke choṭe bhai ki wmər əṭṭhara sal həy.

26.   kəmla ke bəɽe bhai ki wmər tis sal həy.

What have you noticed about these sentences?   What I hope you've noticed is that bhai remains unchanged throughout, or, in other words, that, like ləɽki, the direct and the oblique forms are the same.   But because in all these sentences except 21 and 23 bhai is oblique, and because the adjectives -ka and choṭa and bəɽa end in -a these adjectives do change.   They change -a to -e to agree with the oblique masculine singular noun bhai.

---

1.   H. ve.

əli   ʃəmim   nəsim
                     35   15

11.4   Look at the picture of Ali and his two sisters, and listen to, and read, these sentences:

27.   vwh[1] əli ki choʈi bəhyn həy.

28.   əli ki choʈi bəhyn ka nam nəsim həy.

29.   vwh[1] əli ki bəɽi bəhyn həyŋ.

30.   əli ki bəɽi bəhyn ka nam ʃəmim həy.

31.   əli ki choʈi bəhyn ki wmər pəndra sal həy.

32.   əli ki bəɽi bəhyn ki wmər pəyntis sal həy.

_____

1.   H. ve.

11.5   Now practice talking about the names and ages of your own
and each other's sons and daughters and brothers and sisters.

And now practice talking about the names and ages of your friends'
sons/daughters/brothers/sisters.

At this point I need to say something about the Urdu/Hindi words
for 'friend'.

The general word for friend is <u>dost</u>,[1] and my friend will be <u>mere</u>
<u>dost</u>[1] or <u>meri dost</u>[1] according to whether the friend is male or female.

A woman too may speak of <u>mere dost</u>[1] or <u>meri dost</u>.[1]

But these statements need a good deal of qualifying.

In the traditional South Asian society which Urdu/Hindi usage
reflects a man doesn't <u>have</u> any independent relationship with an adult
woman, and, conversely, no adult woman can have an independent relationship with an adult man.

So a man will call his male friend <u>mere dost</u>[1] while a woman will
call her female friend <u>meri saheli</u>.

In traditional South Asian society, if a man spoke of a woman
as <u>meri dost</u>,[1] he could <u>only</u> mean that he was (shamelessly!) proclaiming
that he and she were lovers; and the same would be the meaning if a
woman spoke of a man as <u>mere dost</u>.[1]

In that society free and informal relationships between adult
men and women are mediated through the menfolk.   Thus a man will speak
to, or of, the wife of a close friend as <u>bhabhi</u>, which really means
'brother's wife'.   Or he might sometimes refer to a woman friend as
his <u>bahyn</u>.

Similarly a woman can have a <u>bhai</u> who isn't a <u>bhai</u> in the
literal sense of the word.

Here in Britain, of course, Urdu/Hindi speakers know that adult
British men and women may be friends without there being anything in
the least improper in the relationship, and where South Asians and
white British people are talking together, and the conversation is
between and/or about people who know, and have a good opinion of, one
another, there's no harm in using <u>dost</u>[1] as synonymous with English
<u>friend</u>.   Outside such a circle, however, it may be wise to tread
rather more carefully!

For practice at this point, women can confine themselves to talking
about the names and ages of the sons/daughters/brothers/sisters of a
<u>saheli</u> and men to those of a <u>dost</u>.[1]

---

1.   H. or, mytr.

Now that you've met all the oblique forms of singular nouns, here is a summary of them:

Summary: oblique forms of singular nouns

masculine	direct	mera/e bhai	mera larka
	oblique	mere bhai (ka, etc.)	mere larke (ka, etc.)
feminine	direct	meri bahyn	meri larki
	oblique	meri bahyn (ka, etc.)	meri larki (ka, etc.)

In short:

Only masculines ending in -a have a different oblique form.

Masculine adjectives ending in -a change the ending to -e to agree with an oblique masculine noun, even if the noun in question (e.g. bhai) doesn't change.

Feminine adjectives end in -i, both for directs and for obliques.

To follow unit 11

(Look at the picture on p. 116)

1. Q.   <u>kəmla</u> ke bəɽe ləɽke ka nam kya həy?

2. A.   <u>kəmla</u> ke bəɽe ləɽke ka nam <u>mohən</u> həy.

3. Q.   <u>kəmla</u> ke choʈe ləɽke ka nam kya həy?

4. A.   <u>kəmla</u> ke choʈe ləɽke ka nam <u>anənd</u> həy.

5. Q.   <u>mohən</u> ki wmər kya həy?

6. A.   <u>mohən</u> ki wmər bara sal həy.

7. Q.   əwr <u>anənd</u> ki wmər kya həy?

8. A.   <u>anənd</u> ki wmər sat sal həy.

(Now look at the picture on p. 119)

9. Q.   <u>əli</u> ki bəɽi ləɽki ka nam kya həy?

10. A.   <u>əli</u> ki bəɽi ləɽki ka nam <u>səmina</u> həy.

11. Q.   <u>əli</u> ki choʈi ləɽki ka nam kya həy?

12. A.   <u>əli</u> ki choʈi ləɽki ka nam <u>fərida</u> həy.

13. Q.   <u>səmina</u> ki wmər kya həy?

14. A.   <u>səmina</u> ki wmər gyara sal həy.

15. Q.   <u>fərida</u> ki wmər kya həy?

16. A.   <u>fərida</u> ki wmər nəw sal həy.

(Now look at the picture on p. 121)

17. Q.   kəmla ke choṭe bhai ka nam kya həy?

18. A.   kəmla ke choṭe bhai ka nam rəvi həy.

19. Q.   kəmla ke bəṛe bhai ka nam kya həy?

20. A.   kəmla ke bəṛe bhai ka nam gopal həy.

21. Q.   rəvi ki wmər kya həy?

22. A.   rəvi ki wmər əṭṭhara sal həy.

23. Q.   gopal ki wmər kya həy?

24. A.   gopal ki wmər tis sal həy.

(Now look at the picture on p.123)

25. Q.   əli ki bəṛi bəhyn ka nam kya həy?

26. A.   əli ki bəṛi bəhyn ka nam ʃəmim həy.

27. Q.   əli ki choṭi bəhyn ka nam kya həy?

28. A.   əli ki choṭi bəhyn ka nam nəsim həy.

29. Q.   ʃəmim ki wmər kya həy?

30. A.   ʃəmim ki wmər pəyntis sal həy.

31. Q.   nəsim ki wmər kya həy?

32. A.   nəsim ki wmər pəndra sal həy.

Unit 12.   More on status, and possessives

Since unit 8 you've had little or no practice on usages
reflecting differences in status, and it seems sensible to return
to these at this point.   One way you can practise this is to talk
about (e.g.) brothers and sisters or children in the age range of,
say 10-16 whom you would (or could) address as twm.   You can't
handle this unless we return to the singular pronouns yyh and vwh
and teach you their possessives.   And it seems sensible while we're
about it to revise all the possessives and to add one or two other
relevant things.

So first re-read unit 8 and then mark for easy reference the
place of page 86, which sets out the complete present tense of rehna
with summary notes on the different pronouns.

Now let's list the possessives.   I'll just give the feminine
form.   You know how to vary it to -a and -e as you need.   The
possessive of:

meyŋ	is	meri	my
ap	is	ap ki	your
twm	is	twmhari	your (addressing a junior)
yyh (sg.)	is	ys ki	his/her (junior, present)
vwh (sg.)	is	ws ki	his/her (junior, absent)
yyh[1]	is	yn ki	his/her (ap status, present)
vwh[2]	is	wn ki	his/her (ap status, absent)
hem	is	hemari	our
yyh[1] (real plural)	is	yn ki	their (present)
vwh[2] (real plural)	is	wn ki	their (absent)

You'll have realised by now that ys, ws, yn and wn are the oblique
forms respectively of yyh (sg.), vwh (sg.), yyh[1] (plu. - real or
courteous) and vwh[2] (plu. - real or courteous).

In case you feel the need to practice using them, here is an
exercise you can do.

---

1.   H. ye.
2.   H. ve.

Practice making simple sentences with possessive pronouns

A. Using a masculine singular noun, such as

məkan	house
ghər	house, home
beṭa	
(choṭa) bhai	
pura nam	full name

make simple sentences using each of the possessive pronouns.
e.g.:

direct form	with possessive pronoun
məyŋ	mera məkan East Oxford meŋ həy. yyh mera choṭa bhai həy.

yyh (present,
    junior,
    e.g. mohən)
	ys ka nam mohən həy.

vwh (absent,
    junior,
    e.g. mera choṭa
      bhai)
	ws ka nam Douglas həy.

həm	yyh həmara məkan həy. həmara məkan Oxford meŋ həy. həmara beṭa skul meŋ həy.
ap	ap ka ghər kəhaŋ həy?
twm	twmhara pura nam kya həy?

yyh (present,
    ap status,
    e.g. Mary)
	yn ka nam Mary həy.

vwh (absent, ap status)	wn ka nam Jonathan həy.

B. **Using a feminine singular noun:**

<u>wmər</u>	
<u>gaṛi</u>	vehicle, car
<u>kar</u>	car
<u>beṭi</u>	
<u>(choṭi) bəhyn</u>	
<u>madri zəban</u>	mother tongue

make simple sentences using each of the possessive pronouns.

e.g.

məyŋ	meri beṭi ghər meŋ həy.
yyh (jun.)	ys ki madri zəban¹ wrdu həy.
vwh (jun.)	ws ki wmər do sal həy.
həm	həmari kar/gaṛi 'garage' meŋ həy.
ap	ap ki madri zəban¹ kya həy?
twm	twmhari wmər kya həy?
yyh (<u>ap</u> status)	yn ki beṭi yskul meŋ həy.
vwh (<u>ap</u> status)	wn ki madri zəban¹ pənjabi həy.

C. Now write out eight sentences with feminine plural nouns, using:

> <u>gaṛiyaŋ</u>
> <u>kareŋ</u>
> <u>beṭiyaŋ</u>
> <u>bəhyneŋ</u>

e.g. meri tin beṭiyaŋ həyŋ.

D. Do the same exercise with masculine plural nouns, using:

> <u>(bəṛe) bhai/do bhai/tin beṭe</u>
> <u>bəcce</u>

e.g.

məyŋ	mere tin bəcce həyŋ.
yyh (jun.)	ys ke bhai bahər gəe həyŋ.
vwh (j.)	(mere choṭe bhai ke tin bəcce həyŋ.)
	<u>ws ke</u> tin bəcce həyŋ.
həm	həmare do bəcce həyŋ.
twm	twmhare kytne bəcce həyŋ?
yyh (<u>ap</u> status)	yn ke kytne bəcce həyŋ?
vwh (<u>ap</u> status)	(mere bəṛe bhai ke tin bəcce həyŋ.)
	<u>wn ke</u> tin bəcce həyŋ.

1. H. matri bhaʃa.

Unit 13.   Schools and homes

This unit introduces oblique plural forms of the four classes of noun. All of them are very similar.   All of them end in -oŋ.

13.1   Listen to, and read, these sentences.   The only words you won't know or guess are dukan 'shop'. and jana, 'to go'.

1.   East Oxford meŋ do sekəndri skul həyŋ.

2.   ləɽke Oxford Boys' skul jate həyŋ.

3.   ləɽkiyaŋ Milham Ford skul jati həyŋ.

4.   ləɽkoŋ ka skul Glanville Road meŋ həy – pakystaniyoŋ ki dukanoŋ ke qərib.

5.   ləɽkiyoŋ ka skul Marston Road ke pas həy, dukanoŋ se dur.

6.   donoŋ skuloŋ meŋ pakystani bəcce həyŋ.

7.   ləɽkiyoŋ ke skul meŋ do wrdu ʈicər həyŋ.

8.   ləɽkoŋ ke skul meŋ koi wrdu ʈicər nəhiŋ həy.

Notes

Note the difference between

ləɽkiyoŋ ka skul – girls' school

and

ləɽkoŋ ka skul – boys' school

Summary: oblique forms of plural nouns

masculine	Direct	bəɽe skul	bəɽe ləɽke
	Oblique	bəɽe skuloŋ meŋ	bəɽe ləɽkoŋ ka
feminine	Direct	bəɽi dukaneŋ	bəɽi ləɽkiyaŋ
	Oblique	bəɽi dukanoŋ meŋ	bəɽi ləɽkiyoŋ ka

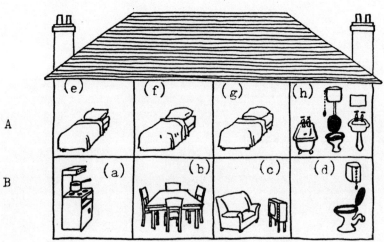

A

B

13.2   <u>Sushila's house</u>

Look at the picture opposite, and listen to, and read, **the**
sentences that follow.

The only words I need to tell/remind you of the meaning of are:

<u>məkan</u> - house

(those of you who did the exercise at the end of unit 12 met it
there) and

<u>kəmra</u> - room

Large or small letters against words in the sentences correspond to
the same letters in the picture, so that, e.g.

<u>ɣwsəlxana</u>$^{h^1}$

will show you that the room with the letter h in it is the <u>ɣwsəlxana</u>,
and will correctly guess that it means 'bathroom'.   Afterwards you
can read the notes to verify your guesses.

9.   yyh <u>swʃila</u> ka məkan həy.

10.   ys məkan meŋ a̧th kəmre həyŋ.

11.   ys ki do mənzyleŋ^{A,B} həyŋ.

12.   nice ki mənzyl^{A}$_{b}$meŋ tin kəmre həyŋ – ek bavəricixana,$^{a^2}$ ek
khane ka kəmra,^{b} əwr ek bəy̧thne ka kəmra.^{c}

13.   ek ţaylət^{d} bhi həy.

14.   upər ki mənzyl^{B} meŋ tin sone ke kəmre^{e,f,g} həyŋ, əwr ek
ɣwsəlxana. $^{h^1}$

---

1.   H. bathrum - many Urdu speakers would also say this.
2.   H. rəsoi/rəsoi-ghər/rəsoi-xana - but in this country many H.
     speakers - and U-speakers - will say kycən.

Notes

9. mǝkan - house

10. kǝmra - room

11. mǝnzyl - floor, storey

12. nice - below

    bavǝrcixana[1] - kitchen.   Here in Britain people will commonly
call it kycǝn.

12. and 14.   khana, bǝythna, sona mean, respectively, to eat, to sit,
to sleep.   But note that the Urdu/Hindi infinitive is sometimes to be
translated (e.g.) 'to eat' and sometimes 'eating'.   So:

12. khane ka kǝmra - dining room ('room of eating')

    bǝythne ka kǝmra - sitting room ('room of sitting')

13. ṭaylet - toilet, lavatory

14. sone ka kǝmra - bedroom ('room of sleeping')

    ɣwsǝlxana - bathroom   (Notice the pronunciation of x)   Here in
Britain people will commonly call it bathrum.

    upǝr - above

    Notice that in listing the vocabulary I have done it in a way
which doesn't tell you the genders.

    Work out from the text of the sentences how you could list the
nouns in the same order, so as to make their gender clear.   Answers
at the bottom of this page, upside down.

---

1.   H. rǝsoi/rǝsoi-ghǝr/rǝsoi-xana - but in this country many H.
    speakers - and U-speakers - will say kycǝn.

1. swʌlla ka mǝkan.   2. kǝmre (or, khane ka kǝmra).   3. mǝnzylẽ.
4, 5, and 6, no clue to the genders of bavǝrcixana, ṭaylet and
ɣwsǝlxana.   These are all masculine.   You could remember them as
chota sa bavǝrcixana, etc. 'smallish kitchen'.

13.3 Jahangir's house, and Paramjit's house

Now look at the second picture, of jəhangir's house, and work out a similar series of sentences about it.

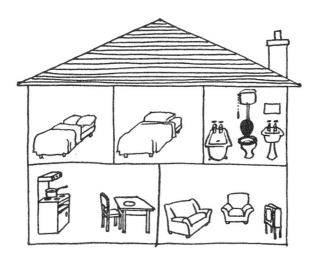

For example: yyh jəhangir ka məkan həy.

ys məkan meŋ paɲc kəmre həyŋ.

Now do the same exercise about the third picture – pərəmjit ka məkan

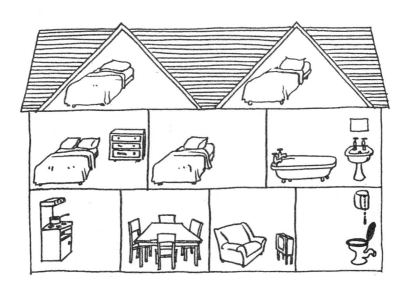

Now work out similar sentences about your own house. Use the word ghər, which means 'home', rather than məkan, which means 'house'. You might need some extra vocabulary:

mere ghər meŋ ek hi mənzyl həy.   (ek hi = just one)

məyŋ fləyt meŋ rəhti huŋ.   (fləyt = flat)

mere fləyt meŋ do sone ke kəmre həyŋ   ....etc.

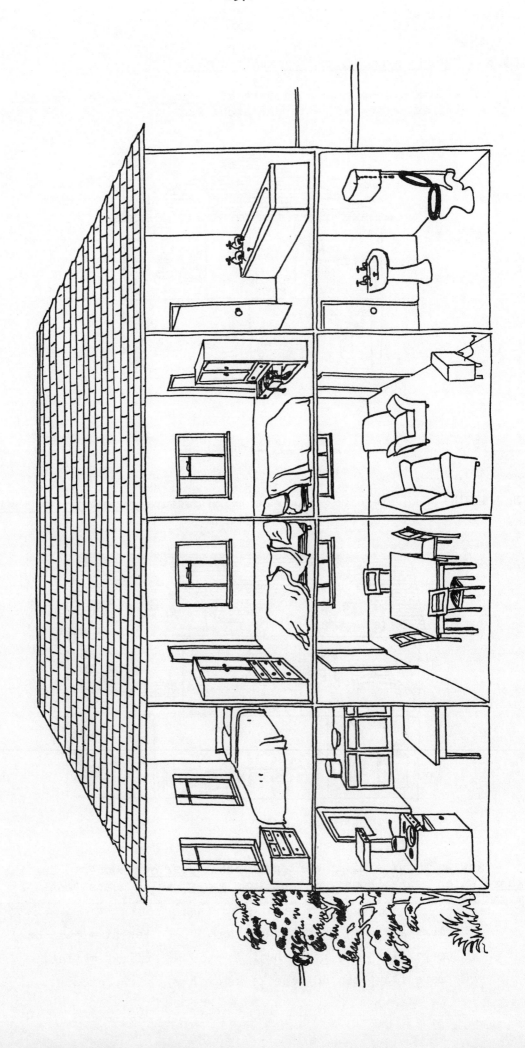

13.4 Sushila's house again

Now look at the full-page picture of the house on the page facing this one, and listen to, and read, these sentences about it.

(yyh meri səheli sw∫ila ka ghər həy.   ys ghər meŋ tin sone ke kəmre həyŋ.)

15. ek sone ka kəmra wn ka əwr wn ke ∫əwhər[1] ka həy.

16. do sone ke kəmre wn ke lərkoŋ ke həyŋ.

17. pəhla kəmra bəɽe lərke ka həy.

18. dusra choʈe lərke ka həy.

19. sw∫ila əwr wn ke ∫əwhər[1] ke sone ke kəmre meŋ do khyɽkiyaŋ həyŋ.

20. khyɽkiyoŋ meŋ se bəɣica nəzər ata həy.

21. ɣwsəlxane[2] ka dərvaza khwla həy.

22. səb dusre kəmroŋ ke dərvaze bənd həyŋ.

English translation of the above

(This is my friend Sushila's house.   In this house [there] are three bedrooms.)

15. One bedroom is hers and her husband's.

16. Two bedrooms are her boys'.

17. The first [bed]room is the elder boy's.

18. The second is the younger boy's.

19. In Sushila and her husband's bedroom [there] are two windows.

20. You can see the garden through the windows. ('From in the windows the garden is visible.')

21. The door of the bathroom is open.

22. The doors of all the other rooms are closed.

---

1. H. pəti.
2. H. (and U.) bathrum.

Notes

From the first sentence in brackets you ought to be able to deduce whether the writer is a man or a woman.   The word <u>saheli</u> should tell you.   If you've forgotten why, look back at p. 125.

<u>pəhla, dusra</u> - 1st, 2nd.

(These are both m. sg. forms.   You had <u>pəhli, dusri</u>, in unit 10, sentence 36.   What would the m.<u>plu</u>. forms be?)

<u>khyrki</u> - window

-<u>men se</u> - 'from in', i.e. (here) through

<u>bayica</u> - garden

<u>nəzər ana</u> - to be visible (written as two words, treated as one)

<u>dərvaza</u> - door

<u>khwla</u> - open

<u>dusra</u> (here, as often) - other

<u>bənd</u> - closed

How would you note the nouns 'bayica' and 'dərvaza' to show you their gender?

Now work out similar sentences about your own house.

e.g.   həmare ghər men tin sone ke kəmre həyn,   etc.

13.5   Describing one's own house

If you wanted to ask someone to describe her/his house to you in similar detail you would say

<u>əpne ghər ki təfsil[1] bətaiye</u>

<u>təfsil</u>[1] means 'detail', and is usually used to mean detail<u>s</u> too. Notice the <u>əpne</u>.

<u>əpna, əpni, əpne</u> can mean <u>any</u> of the possessive pronouns -

my,   your,   his,   her,   their

---

1.   H. ka byora.

and it <u>must</u> be used when it refers to the subject of the sentence.
So

       Bashir took me to his house

can be translated

    1. <u>baʃir mwjhe əpne ghər legəe</u>

          or

    2. <u>baʃir mwjhe wn ke ghər legəe</u>

but in sentence 1 the house is Bashir's own house and in sentence 2 it is someone else's.

<u>lejana</u> (past <u>legəya</u>) means 'to take' in the sense of to take someone or something somewhere.

So also in the sentences

     <u>məyŋ əpne dost ke məkan meŋ rəhta huŋ</u>

and   <u>vwh mere məkan meŋ rəhta həy</u>

the <u>əpne</u> and the <u>mere</u> both mean 'my', but the first sentence demands <u>əpne</u> – (<u>mere</u> would be quite wrong) – because the <u>my</u> refers to the subject of the sentence, whereas in the second sentence it doesn't.

13.6 Sushila's house once more

Now as a final exercise look again at the full-page picture and listen to, and read, these sentences:

23. səb sone ke kəmroŋ meŋ əlmariyaŋ həyŋ.

24. ləɽkoŋ ke sone ke kəmroŋ meŋ bəɽi əlmariyaŋ həyŋ.

25. <u>swʃila</u> əwr <u>rəjeʃ</u> ke kəmre meŋ choʈi əlmari həy.

26. tinoŋ əlmariyoŋ meŋ dərazeŋ həyŋ.

27. donoŋ bəɽi əlmariyoŋ meŋ tin dərazeŋ həyŋ, əwr choʈi əlmari meŋ car dərazeŋ həyŋ.

28. ləɽkoŋ ki ek əlmari ki ek dəraz khwli həy.

29. ys dəraz meŋ ləɽkoŋ ke moze həyŋ.

English translation of the above

23. In all the bedrooms [there] are cupboards.

24. In the boys' bedrooms [there] are big cupboards.

25. In Sushila and Rajesh's bedroom [there] is a small cupboard.

26. In all three cupboards there are drawers.

27. In both the big cupboards [there] are three drawers, and in the little cupboard [there] are four drawers.

28. One drawer of one of the boys' cupboard ('of the boys' one cupboard') is open.

29. In this drawer [there] are the boy's socks.

Notes

əlmari - cupboard

dəraz - draw

moza - sock

How would you note these words in a way that tells you their gender?

Now read the description of Sushila's house in sentences 9-29 on pages 134, 138 and 140.

Summary

Direct and oblique forms of nouns, and agreement of adjectives

		Singular	Plural
masc. in -a	Direct	mera beʈa	mere beʈe
	Oblique	mere beʈe (ka, etc.)	mere beʈoŋ (ka)
masc. not in -a	Direct	mera bhai	mere bhai
	Oblique	mere bhai (ka)	mere bhaiyoŋ (ka)
fem. in -i	Direct	meri beʈi	meri beʈiyaŋ
	Oblique	meri beʈi (ka)	meri beʈiyoŋ (ka)
fem. not in -i	Direct	meri bəhyn	meri bəhyneŋ
	Oblique	meri bəhyn (ka)	meri bəhynoŋ (ka)

To follow unit 13

1. Q. sw∫ila ke məkan meŋ kytne kəmre hayŋ?

2. A. sw∫ila ke məkan men sat kəmre həyŋ.

3. Q. ws ki kytni mənzyleŋ həyŋ?

4. A. Ws ki do mənzyleŋ həyŋ.

5. Q. nice ki mənzyl meŋ kytne kəmre həyŋ? wn ki təfsil[1] bətaiye.

6. A. nice ki mənzyl meŋ tin kəmre hayŋ - ek bavərcixana,[2] ek khane ka kəmra, əwr ek bəyţhne ka kəmra. ek ţaylət bhi həy.

7. Q. upər ki mənzyl meŋ kytne kəmre həyŋ? təfsil[3] bətaiye.

8. A. upər ki mənzyl meŋ tin sone ke kəmre həyŋ, əwr ek ɣwsəlxana.[4]

9. Q. sone ke kəmroŋ ki təfsil[1] bətaiye.

10. A. ek sone ka kəmra wn ka əwr wn ke ∫əwhər[5] ka həy. do sone ke kəmre wn ke ləɽkoŋ ke həyŋ. pəhla bəɽe ləɽke ka həy. dusra choţe ləɽke ka həy.

11. Q. sw∫ila əwr wn ke ∫əwhər[5] ke sone ke kəmre meŋ kytni khyɽkiyəŋ həyŋ?

12. A. do khyɽkiyəŋ həyŋ.

13. Q. khyɽkiyoŋ meŋ se bəɣica nəzər ata həy?

14. A. ji haŋ, nəzər ata həy.

15. Q. ɣwsəlxane[4] ka dərvaza khwla həy, ya bənd həy?

16. A. ɣwsəlxane[4] ka dərvaza khwla həy.

17. Q. səb dusre kəmroŋ ke dərvaze bənd həyŋ?

18. A. ji haŋ, səb dusre kəmroŋ ke dərvaze bənd həyŋ.

19. Q. sone ke kəmroŋ meŋ kytni əlmariyəŋ həyŋ?

20. A. tin əlmariyəŋ həyŋ.

---

1. H. ka byora.
2. See note 2 on p.134.
3. H. byora.
4. H. (and U.) bathrum.
5. H. pəti.

21. Q. sw∫ila əwr rəje∫ ke kəmre ki əlmari meŋ kytni dərazeŋ
         həyŋ?

22. A. car dərazeŋ həyŋ.

23. Q. ləɾkoŋ ki ek əlmari ki ek dəraz khwli həy.   ws dəraz meŋ
         kya həy?

24. A. ws dəraz meŋ ləɾkoŋ ke moze həyŋ.

Unit 14.   Knowing languages

14.1   Knowing languages

Listen to, and read, the following dialogue, set out on the next page.   I shall give you only a few preliminary notes - enough for you to follow the dialogue without much difficulty - and, as before, you can study the detailed notes afterwards.

-ko is used in several senses, but most commonly it means 'to'. Already in unit 2 you met

> ap ko malum həy?

meaning 'Is [it] known to you?' - i.e. Do you know?

and

> ap ko yad həy?

meaning 'Is [it] remembered to you?' - i.e. Do you remember.

Another very common use is with ana, 'to come'.

> ap ko wrdu ati həy?
> 'Does Urdu come to you?'

is the regular way of asking 'Do you know Urdu?' or 'Do you speak Urdu?'.

You will hear this a lot in the dialogue.

Make sure you remember what the Urdu/Hindi sentence literally means.   When an Urdu/Hindi sentence differs in structure from its natural English equivalent, remembering the literal translation will help you to get it right when you speak.

Towards the end of the dialogue you will hear the sentence

> ap wn ko janti həyŋ?

which means, 'Do you know him?' - and in this sentence wn ko simply means 'him' and ko has no English word to correspond to it.   In the next unit you will be learning a lot more about this.

1. Sue   məyŋ wrdu sikh rəhi huŋ, əwr əb mwjhe thoɽi si wrdu
          ati həy.   ap ko wrdu ati həy?

2. Habib ji haŋ, mwjhe wrdu ati həy.   ap ko əwr koi zəban[1]
          ati həy?

3. S.   ji haŋ, mwjhe əngrezi ati həy.   əngrezi meri madri
          zəban[2] həy.   əwr thoɽi si fransisi bhi ati həy.   ap
          pakystan meŋ kəhaŋ rəhte the?

4. H.   məyŋ jəhlwm meŋ rəhta tha.

5. S.   əccha.   ap ko pənjabi bhi ati həy?

6. H.   ji haŋ, mwjhe pənjabi bhi ati həy.

7. S.   ap ki beʈi ko wrdu ati həy, ya pənjabi - ya donoŋ zəbaneŋ?[3]

8. H.   ws ko donoŋ zəbaneŋ[3] ati həyŋ.   vwh ghər meŋ pənjabi bolti
          həy, əwr ws ko thoɽi si wrdu bhi ati həy.   vwh skul meŋ
          wrdu pəɽhti həy.   əngrezi bhi ati həy.

9. S.   ap ke beʈe ko bhi wrdu ati həy?

10. H.   ji nəhiŋ, vwh skul meŋ wrdu nəhiŋ pəɽhta, əwr ghər meŋ
          wrdu nəhiŋ bolta.   ws ko syrf pənjabi ati həy, əwr thoɽi
          si əngrezi.

11. S.   əccha.   ap ko pəʃto ati həy?

12. H.   ji nəhiŋ, mwjhe pəʃto nəhiŋ ati.

13. S.   kəwn log pəʃto bolte həyŋ?

14. H.   pəʈhan log pəʃto bolte həyŋ.   <u>əsləm xan</u> pəʈhan həyŋ.   ap
          wn ko janti həyŋ?

15. S.   ji haŋ, wn ko janti huŋ.   vwh əcchi əngrezi bhi bolte
          həyŋ, əwr wrdu bhi jante həyŋ.   əccha, wn ko pəʃto bhi
          ati həy?

16. H.   ji haŋ, pəʈhan həyŋ; sərhəd ke həyŋ.

          <u>England</u> ane se pəhle pyʃavər meŋ rəhte the.

---

1. H. bhaʃa.
2. H. matri bhaʃa.
3. H. bhaʃaeŋ.

Notes on the dialogue

1.   sikh rəhi huŋ - am learning.   Here for the first time you
meet the form of the present tense which describes what is actually
going on at the present time.

> məyŋ swnti huŋ
> I listen
>
> məyŋ swn rəhi huŋ
> I am listening
>
> həm kəhte həyŋ
> we say
>
> həm kəh rəhe həyŋ
> we are saying
>
> twm skul jate ho?
> Do you go to school?
>
> twm skul ja rəhe ho?
> Are you going to school?

As you see, the root is followed by rəha/rəhi huŋ, rəhe/rəhi
həyŋ and so on, with the rəha, -i, -e changing on exactly the same
pattern as (e.g.) in other tenses rəhta changes to rəhti/rəhte.

In this present continuous sense rəha, -i -e is to be regarded
simply as a piece of the machinery which shows that it is this tense.
There's no point in speculating on why this particular word is used
for this purpose.

The corresponding past tense is formed, as you'd perhaps expect
by now, by substituting tha, thi, the, thiŋ for huŋ, həy, həyŋ, etc.

I will set these tenses out in a table at the end of this unit.

1.   thoɽa sa - 'a little-ish', a little (in quantity).   (Like choṭa
sa - little (in size) in unit 4, sentence 23).

The thoɽi si tells you that 'wrdu' is feminine.

All languages are feminine, because zəban[1] is feminine. zəban[2]
means 'tongue' both in the literal and in the figurative sense - i.e.
it means both the thing in your mouth and the 'tongue', or language,
you speak with it.

2.   əwr koi - 'other any', any other.   This use of əwr is common.
The order koi əwr is also O.K.

---

1. H. bhaʃa.
2. but not bhaʃa.

əngrezi - English.   Note that əngrezi is used for (1) the language, and (2) things.   An English person is əngrez - without the i at the end.

madri zəban[1] - mother tongue

fransisi - French

8. bolna - to speak

pərhna - to read.   Also, as here, to study, learn.

10. syrf - only

13. kəwn log? - 'who people'?, which people?   Notice that log is masculine plural.

14. janna - to know.   (More on this later.)

On the next page is a natural English translation of the dialogue. See if, without looking at the original, you can translate it back into Urdu/Hindi.   Remember that 'Do you know Urdu?' or 'Do you speak Urdu?' will become

Does Urdu come to you?

When you've done it, check very carefully.   Where you've written something different from the original it won't necessarily be wrong; don't assume either that it is or that it isn't;   but at this stage stick closely to the model you have on the yellow page.   It's a good idea to work with a partner, learn the dialogue, and act it out with her/him, one of you speaking Sue's part, and one of you Habib's.

Then do the same exercise, but adapting the dialogue to one which you might speak with a Panjabi/Hindi speaker rather than a Panjabi/Urdu speaker.   To do this you could make the following substitutions:

Rajindar (rajyndər)	for	Habib
Hindi	"	Urdu
India	"	Pakistan
Jullundar (jaləndhər)	"	Jhelum
Gujarati	"	Pashto
Gujaratis	"	Pathan people
Dipak Patel (dipək pəṭel)	"	Asləm Khan
Gujarati	"	Pathan
Gujarat state (prədeṣ)	"	the Frontier
Baroda (bəroḍa)	"	Peshawar

You'll also need to use the Hindi words (given in the notes above) for 'language' - 'mother tongue'.

───────────

1. H. matri bhaṣa.

English translation of the dialogue:

1.   Sue   I am learning Urdu, and now I know a little Urdu.
Do you know Urdu?

2.   Habib Yes, I know Urdu.   Do you know any other language?

3.   S.   Yes, I know English.   English is my mother tongue. And
I know a little French too.   Where did you live in
Pakistan?

4.   H.   I lived in Jhelum.

5.   S.   I see.   Do you know Panjabi too?

6.   H.   Yes, I know Panjabi too.

7.   S.   Does your daughter know Urdu, or Panjabi - or both
languages?

8.   H.   She knows both languages.   She speaks Panjabi at home
and she knows a little Urdu too.   She studies Urdu in
school.   She knows English too.

9.   S.   Does your son too know Urdu?

10.   H.   No, he doesn't study Urdu at school and doesn't speak Urdu
at home.   He knows only Panjabi and a little English.

11.   S.   I see.   Do you know Pashto?

12.   H.   No, I don't know Pashto.

13.   S.   Who speaks Pashto?

14.   H.   The Pathan people speak Pashto.   <u>əsləm xan</u> is a Pathan.
Do you know him?

15.   S.   Yes, I know him.   He speaks good English too, and he
knows Urdu too.   So he knows Pashto?

16.   H.   Yes, he does.   He is a Pathan; he is from the Frontier.
Before coming to England he lived in Peshawar.

14.2   Now work out statements about what languages you and your friends know, and work out what questions would be asked to elicit this information.   Here is some extra vocabulary you may need.

ap ki madri zəban[1] kya həy? - What's your mother tongue?

jərmən - German

yspəyny∫ - Spanish

yṭəylyən - Italian

bəngali - Bengali

hyndi - Hindi

ərəbi - Arabic

farsi - Persian

14.3   'To know'

You know now that 'knowing' is expressed in several ways.

1.   Using malum, 'known'

mwjhe malum həy
'to me known is', I know

2.   Using ana, 'to come'

mwjhe wrdu ati həy
'To me Urdu comes', I know Urdu

This is used to knowledge of languages, and also of skills.

mwjhe khana pəkana ata həy
'To me food-cooking comes', I can cook

3.   Using janna, 'to know'

You can use janna for 1 and 2 above as well.

məyŋ janta huŋ = mwjhe malum həy

məyŋ khana pəkana janta huŋ = mwjhe khana pəkana ata həy

But it is most commonly used of knowing people - as in sentences 14 and 15 of the dialogue.

_____

1.   H. matri bha∫a.

151.

To follow unit 14

1. Q. ap ki madri zəban^1 kya həy?

2. A. meri madri zəban^1 .... həy.

3. Q. ap ko koi əwr zəban^2 ati həy?

4. A. ji nəhiŋ, koi əwr zəban^2 nəhiŋ ati.

       _or_

       ji həŋ, ... ati həy. .. bhi ati həy. thoɽi si ....
bhi ati həy.

5. Q. (to W) ap koi əwr zəban^2 sikh rəhi həyŋ?

6. A. ji həŋ, ⌊məyŋ⌋ wrdu/hyndi sikh rəhi huŋ.

7. Q. bəngali zəban^2 kəwn log bolte həyŋ?

8. A. bəngali zəban^2 bəngladeʃi bolte həyŋ, əwr bharət ke bəngali
bhi bolte həyŋ.

9. Q. sykh kya zəban^2 bolte həyŋ? ap ko malum həy?

10. A. ji həŋ, ⌊mwjhe⌋ malum həy. sykh pənjabi bolte həyŋ.

11. Q. (to W) ap kysi sykh ko janti həyŋ? ap ki koi səheli sykh
həyŋ?

12. A. ji nəhiŋ, məyŋ kysi sykh ko nəhiŋ janti ⌊huŋ⌋.

       _or_

       ji həŋ, meri ek səheli sykh həyŋ.

       _or_

       ji həŋ, meri .... səheliyəŋ sykh həyŋ.

13. Q. ap ko khana pəkana ata həy?

14. A. ji həŋ, ata həy.

---

1. H. matri bhaʃa.
2. H. bhaʃa.

Unit 15. Whom do you know?

In unit 6 , in passing, you met the sentence

təsvir nəmbər ek ko dekhiye

and were told that in this sentence -ko doesn't correspond to any English word but simply indicates that təsvir nəmbər ek is the object of dekhiye.

In unit 14, sentence 14 you met wn ko meaning 'him' - i.e. another example of -ko simply marking the object.

Now listen to, and read, this dialogue.   There are not many words you don't know, and some of these you'll easily guess.   Don't bother about the others.   Get the general sense, and look at the notes afterwards.

1. A. aj nəsim mere ghər a rəhi həyŋ.   vwh meri səheli həyŋ. bəhwt əcchɪ əwrət[1] həyŋ.   ap wn ko jante həyŋ?

2. B. ji nəhiŋ, wn ko nəhiŋ janta.   syddiq ko - wn ke ʃəwhər[2] ko - janta huŋ.   ap wn ko janti həyŋ?

3. A. ji nəhiŋ, məyŋ wn ko nəhiŋ janti.

4. B. ap nasyr ko janti həyŋ?

5. A. ji həŋ, nasyr ko janti huŋ.

6. B. syddiq wn ke bhai həyŋ.

7. A. əccha?   yyh mwjhe nəhiŋ malum tha.   syddiq əwr nasyr səge bhai həyŋ?

8. B. ji nəhiŋ, həqiqi[3] bhai nəhiŋ, səge bhai nəhiŋ.   syddiq nasyr ke cəca-zad[4] bhai həyŋ.

9. A. əccha.   ap syddiq ko kəyse jante həyŋ?

10. B. həm donoŋ British Leyland meŋ kam kərte həyŋ.   wn ko do sal se janta huŋ.   bəhwt əcche admi həyŋ.

11. A. əccha.   ap bəccoŋ ko bhi jante həyŋ? — dekhiye, nəsim a rəhi həyŋ.   wn ki lərki wn ke sath həy.   lərki ka nam əmina həy.

---

1. H. or, stri.
2. H. pəti.
3. H. səge.
4. H. cəcera.

12. B.   mwjhe malum həy...ji haŋ, bəccoŋ ko janta huŋ.   wn
             ke do bəcce həyŋ, yyh ləɾki, əwr ek ləɾka ənvər. ek dəfa
             vwh syddiq ke sath mere ghər ae.   bəhwt pyare bəcce həyŋ...
             əmina nəsim ke sath a rəhi həy.   ənvər kəhaŋ həy?

13. A.   ənvər skul jata həy.   əb ws ki wmər pəŋc sal həy.

14. B.   əccha?   yyh mwjhe nəhiŋ malum tha.

Notes on the dialogue

1.   aj - today

    mere ghər - can you guess why it's mere?   (Answer upside down at the bottom of the page.)

    əwrət[1] - you had the plural of this as early as unit 1.   What is it?

7.   yyh - 'this', where English would say 'that'.

7,8.   səga and həqiqi[2] are both used to distinguish a 'real' brother. (i.e. a brother in the strict sense of the word) from cousins, whom South Asians commonly call 'brother', as you were told in unit

    Similarly səgi bəhyn, həqiqi bəhyn[2] = sister (as opposed to cousin).

8.   cəca-zad[3] - 'uncle born'.   Your cəca is your father's younger brother.   There are many other words for 'uncle' - one each for each kind.   You'll find them all listed in Part II of this Course.

9.   kəyse? - how?

10.   admi - 'a descendant of adəm - i.e. Adam.'   In standard Urdu it can be used both for a man and for a woman.   In Hindi, and in the Urdu of most Panjabi speakers, it always means a man.

11.   -ke sath - with

12.   ek dəfa - one time, once

13.   pyara - literally 'dear', but here just 'nice'.

It means 'to my house'.   You know that in Urdu/Hindi you say ghər meyn ja rahi hun, without any postposition (just as we say 'I'm going home'), and meyn ləndan gəya, I went [to] London, and meyn dəftar pəhunci hun, I arrive [at] the office (see unit 9, sentence 5), also without any postposition.   But a postposition is implied; so ghər is oblique, and mere oblique in agreement with it.

---

1.   H. or, stri.
2.   H. only səga, not həqiqi.
3.   H. cəcere (m. sg. cəcera).

Here is a natural English translation of this dialogue. Do the same exercise on it as you did on the dialogue in unit 15.

1. A. Today nəsim is coming to my house. She's my friend. She's a very nice (literally, 'good') woman. Do you know her?

2. B. No, I don't know her. I know syddiq, her husband. Do you know him?

3. A. No, I don't know him.

4. B. Do you know nasyr?

5. A. Yes, I know nasyr.

6. B. syddiq is his brother.

7. A. Really? I didn't know that. Are syddiq and nasyr 'real' brothers?

8. B. No, not 'real' brothers, not 'true' brothers. syddiq is nasyr's cousin ('uncle-born brother').

9. A. I see. How do you know syddiq?

10. B. We both work in British Leyland. I've known him for two years. He's a very nice man.

11. A. I see. Do you know the children too? - Look, nəsim's coming. Her girl (i.e. daughter) is with her. The girl's name is əmina.

12. B. I know... Yes, I know the children. They've got two children, this girl, and a boy, ənvər. They came once with syddiq to my house. They're very nice children... əmina's coming with nəsim. Where's ənvər?

13. A. ənvər goes to school. He's five now.

14. B. Really? I didn't know that.

You'll have seen that in this dialogue practically every time
-ko occurs it simply marks the object of the sentence.   You can't
devise any easy rule which would tell you when to express the object
with -ko and when to use the direct form, but when a pronoun (me,
you, him, her, it, us, them) is the object of the sentence it nearly
always has -ko with it;   and -ko is also very often used when the
object is a person.

All pronouns with -ko except ap also have single-word forms
which are interchangeable with the oblique - plus -ko.   Most, but
not all, pronouns have a separate oblique form.

Here is the full list.

Direct	Oblique with ko	One-word equivalent
məyŋ	mwjh ko	mwjhe
yyh (sing.)	ys ko	yse
vwh (sing.)	ws ko	wse
həm	həm ko	həmeŋ
twm	twm ko	twmheŋ
ap	ap ko	-
yyh[1] (plu.)	yn ko	ynheŋ
yyh[2] (plu.)	wn ko	wnheŋ

You'll find it helpful to practice using these forms from time
to time until you are thoroughly familiar with all of them.   So
on the next two pages I have drawn up two lists, one in English and one in
Urdu/Hindi.   In the first column is a list of pronouns and nouns to
be used as subjects of the sentences.   In the second column is the
verb 'know/knows'.   And in the third is again a list of pronouns and
nouns to be used as the object, in every case to be expressed with -ko
or the one-word equivalent of the pronoun - plus -ko.   Use this
list to practice making different sentences.   On the page following
I give you the Urdu/Hindi equivalents, numbered to correspond with the
numbers on the preceding page, so that you can check whether you've
got your Urdu/Hindi versions right.

---

1.   H. ye.
2.   H. ve.

1.	I	know,	1.	me	
2.	you (junior)	knows	2.	you (junior)	
3.	you (equal)		3.	you (equal)	
4.	he (equal and present)		4.	him (equal and present)	
5.	he (junior and present)		5.	him (junior and present)	
6.	he (equal and not present)		6.	him (equal and not present)	
7.	he (junior and not present)		7.	him (junior and not present)	
8.	she (equal and present)		8.	her (equal and present)	
9.	she (junior and present)		9.	her (junior and present)	
10.	she (equal and not present)		10.	her (equal and not present)	
11.	she (junior and not present)		11.	her (junior and not present)	
12.	we		12.	us	
13.	they (present, m. or mixed)		13.	them (present)	
14.	they (not present, m. or mixed)		14.	them (not present)	
15.	they (present, f.)		15.	the younger boy	
16.	they (not present, f.)		16.	the younger girl	
17.	my [younger] brother		17.	the younger boys	
18.	my brothers		18.	the younger girls	
19.	my son		19.	the younger brother	
20.	my sons		20.	the younger sister	
21.	my sister		21.	the younger brothers	
22.	my sisters		22.	the younger sisters	
23.	my daughter				
24.	my daughters				

Here is the total possible range of variations which you will
use in translating the sentences constructed from the three columns
on the previous page.   So that you can check, I have numbered the
entries in cols. 1 and 2 on this page to correspond with those in
cols. 1 and 3 of the previous page.   Obviously I can't number the
entries in the other column, because you have to select from a number
of different Urdu/Hindi forms to translate a single English form.

1.	məyŋ	1. mwjh ko, mwjhe	janta huŋ
2.	twm	2. twm ko, twmheŋ	janti huŋ
3.	ap	3. ap ko	janta həy
4.	yyh[1]	5,9. ys ko, yse	janti həy
5.	yyh	7,11. ws ko, wse	jante həyŋ
6.	vwh[2]	4,8,13. yn ko, ynheŋ	janti həyŋ
7.	vwh	6,10,14. wn ko, wnheŋ	jante ho
8.	yyh[1]	12. həm ko, həmeŋ	janti ho
9.	yyh	15. choʈe ləɾke ko	
10.	vwh[2]	16. choʈi ləɾki ko	
11.	vwh	17. chote ləɾkoŋ ko	
12.	həm	18. choʈi lərkiyoŋ ko	
13,15.	yyh[1]	19. chote bhai ko	
14,16.	vwh[2]	20. choʈi bəhyn ko	
17.	mera bhai	21. choʈe bhaiyoŋ ko	
18.	mere bhai	22. choʈi bəhynoŋ ko	
19.	mera beʈa		
20.	mere beʈe		
21.	meri bəhyn		
22.	meri bəhyneŋ		
23.	meri beʈi		
24.	meri beʈiyəŋ		

---

1. H. ye.
2. H. ve.

Unit 16. Today, tomorrow and yesterday
Days of the week

In this unit you're going to learn the future tense.

16.1   Getting up tomorrow

Listen to, and read, this short dialogue about what time various people are going to get up tomorrow.   (kəl means 'tomorrow'.) All the verb forms that end in -ga, -gi or -ge are futures.   There's a bit more to it than that, though, and the notes that follow the dialogue will make this clear.

1.   M.   kəl məyŋ sat bəje wṭhuŋga.   ap kytne bəje wṭheŋgi?

2.   W.   məyŋ bhi sat bəje wṭhuŋgi.

3.   M.   əwr yyh?[1]   yyh[1] kytne bəje wṭheŋge?

4.   W.   mera xəyal həy ky yyh[1] səva sat, saṛhe sat bəje wṭheŋge.

5.   M.   əwr bəcce?   yyh[2] kytne bəje wṭheŋge?

6.   W.   malum nəhiŋ.   kəl chwṭṭi hogi.   ənvər, kəl kytne bəje wṭhoge?

7.   Anwar. saṛhe aṭh bəje wṭhuŋga.   chwṭṭi həy, na?

8.   W.   əwr əmina, twm?   twm kytne bəje wṭhogi?

9.   Amina. pəta nəhiŋ ... saṛhe aṭh, pəwne nəw...

Notes

mera xəyal həy ky... - '⌊it⌋ is my thought that'..., 'I think that...'

chwṭṭi hogi - 'holiday will be'

   kəl chwṭṭi hogi - Tomorrow's a holiday

pəta nəhiŋ is a rather off-hand malum nəhiŋ.

---

1.   H. ye.
2.   H. ve.

English translation

1. **M.**   Tomorrow I shall get up at 7 o'clock.   What time will you (f.) get up?

2. **W.**   I too shall get up at 7 o'clock.

3. **M.**   And he?   What time will he get up?

4. **W.**   I think he'll get up at a quarter past or half past 7.

5. **M.**   And the children?   What time will they get up?

6. **W.**   I don't know.   Tomorrow's a holiday.   Anwar, what time will you get up?

7. **Anwar**   I'll get up at half past 8.   It's a holiday, isn't it.

8. **W.**   And Amina, you?   What time will you get up?

9. **Amina**   I don't know.. half past 8, a quarter to nine....

The short dialogue exemplifies all the future tense forms.
Here is the future tense of wṭhna set out in full:

Feminine forms

məyŋ wṭhuŋgi	I shall get up
[tu wṭhegi]	[thou **wilt get up**]
yyh wṭhegi	she[1,2] will get up
vwh wṭhegi	she[3,2] will get up
həm wṭheŋge[4]	we shall get up
ap wṭheŋgi	you will get up
twm wṭhogi	you[2] will get up
yyh[5] wṭheŋgi	they[1] will get up
	she[1,7] will get up
vwh[6] wṭheŋgi	they[3] will get up
	she[3,7] will get up

Masculine forms *

məyŋ wṭhuŋga	I shall get up
[tu wṭhega]	[thou wilt get up]
yyh wṭhega	he[1,2] will get up
vwh wṭhega	he[3,2] will get up
həm wṭheŋge	we shall get up
ap wṭheŋge	you will get up
twm wṭhoge	you[2] will get up
yyh[5] wṭheŋge	they[1] will get up
	he[1,7] will get up
vwh[6] wṭheŋge	they[3] will get up
	he[3,7] will get up

As you see, the -uŋga/-uŋgi, -ega/egi, -oge/ogi and -eŋge/eŋgi
endings are tacked on to the root. You can make the future of practically
all verbs in this way. Thus the future of rəhna, to live, will be

     məyŋ rəhuŋgi/a   etc.

---

1. present.
2. junior status.
3. absent.
4. H., and many Panjabi speakers: wṭheŋgi.
5. H. ye.
6. H. ve.
7. ap status.

---

* The masculine plural forms are also used for mixed m. and f.
subjects.

16.2   <u>Practice</u>

Now look back at unit 9.   Take the sentences of the first
short piece describing Jamila's daily routine, and turn them all
into statements of what she will do tomorrow.   It should give you
no problems at all - but you need one piece of guidance.

The future equivalent of <u>nykəlti həy</u> will not be "nykəlegi" but

<u>nyklegi</u>.

In Urdu/Hindi, where the last letter but one of the root of a
verb is <u>ə</u> it is dropped before any ending that begins with a vowel.

So

<u>nykəlna</u> - 'to emerge', come out, go out

Root <u>nykəl</u>.

<u>məyŋ nykəlti huŋ</u> - I go out

<u>məyŋ nykəlti thi</u> - I used to go out

<u>məyŋ nykəl rəhi huŋ</u> - I am going out

But

<u>məyŋ nykli</u> - I went out

<u>məyŋ nykli huŋ</u> - I have gone out

<u>məyŋ nykluŋgi</u> - I shall go out

If you want more practice, do the same exercise with some (or
even all!) of the sentences in the dialogue on pp.91-92 of unit 9.

16.3   <u>Days of the week.   'Will be' and 'was'</u>

Listen to, and then read, the dialogue on the next page.   It's
designed to teach you the days of the week in Urdu, and therefore isn't
the kind of natural conversational exchange you'd have in real life, so
to speak - unless you were asking someone to test your knowledge of the
days of the week.

At the end of the dialogue I give you such notes as you need to
be able to follow it, but I don't give the names of any of the days
except Friday.   If you find that you can't manage to register the others
without seeing them in writing, turn to page 165, where I've listed them.

On that page I also list the corresponding Hindi names, and if
it's these you need you should have this list before you as you listen,
because you won't be hearing them in the recording.   I also explain on
that page who uses which names, and why.

10. A.   swniye: aj jwma^1 həy.   <u>June</u>, ap bətaiye, aj kya dyn həy?

11. J.   aj jwma^1 həy.

12. A.   țhik həy, aj jwma^1 həy.   əb swniye: kəl həfta^2, ya sənicər,^{2} hoga.   <u>Ann</u>, ap bətaiye, kəl kya dyn hoga?

13. Ann. kəl həfta,^{2} ya sənicər^2 hoga.

14. A.   țhik həy, kəl həfta^2 hoga - ya sənicər.^{2} əb bətaiye - <u>Ken</u>, ap bətaiye, pərsoŋ kya dyn hoga?

15. K.   pərsoŋ ytvar^3 hoga.

16. A.   ji haŋ, əwr ws ke bad kya dyn hoga?   <u>Margaret</u>, ap bətaiye.

17. M.   ws ke bad pir^4 hoga.

18. A.   ji haŋ, pir^4 hoga.   əwr ws ke bad?   <u>Brian</u>, ap bətaiye.

19. B.   ws ke bad məngəl^5 hoga.

20. A.   əwr məngəl^5 ke bad?   <u>Kate</u>?

21. K.   məngəl^5 ke bad bwdh^6 hoga.

22. A.   əwr bwdh^6 ke bad?   <u>Tom</u>?

23. T.   bwdh^6 ke bad jwmerat^7 hogi.

24. A.   ji haŋ, jwmerat^7 <u>hogi</u>.   ʃabaʃ!   əwr ws ke bad kya dyn hoga?   <u>Terry</u>?

25. T.   ws ke bad jwma^1 hoga.

26. A.   ji haŋ.   əwr aj kya dyn həy?   <u>June</u>?

27. J.   aj jwma^1 həy.

28. A.   əwr kəl kya dyn tha?   <u>Kate</u>?

29. K.   kəl jwmerat^7 thi - əwr pərsoŋ bwdh^6 tha, əwr ws se pəhle məngəl^5 tha, əwr ws se pəhle pir^4 tha, əwr pir^4 se pəhle ytvar^3 tha, əwr ytvar^3 se pəhle həfta^2 tha, ya sənicər,^{2} əwr ws se pəhle jwma^1 tha.

30. A.   bəhwt əccha!   ʃabaʃ!

---

1.   H. ʃwkrəvar.
2.   H. ʃənivar.
3.   H. or, rəvivar.
4.   H. somvar.
5.   H. məngəlvar.
6.   H. bwdhvar.
7.   H. bryhəspətivar, or gwruvar.   These are masculine, so the verb will be <u>hoga</u>.

Notes

hona, 'to be' (and a few other verbs) have a sort of telescoped form of the future. Thus:

hoga/hogi - will be

The only other notes you need for the moment are these:

tha/thi - was

aj - today

kəl (with a future verb) - tomorrow

kəl (with a past verb) - yesterday

pərsoŋ (with a future verb) - the day after tomorrow

pərsoŋ (with a past verb) - the day before yesterday

jwma[1] - Friday

-ke bad - after-

ws ke bad - after that

jwme[1] ke bad - after Friday

-se pəhle - before-

ws se pəhle - before that

jwme[1] se pəhle - before Friday

With this information you should be able to work out from the dialogue the other days of the week. Note that one of them is feminine, and this puts the verb in the feminine form.

---

1.   H. ʃwkrəvar.

Urdu and Hindi days of the week

The days of the week are called by different names reflecting the religious/cultural background of the speaker. Here they are:

	Urdu	Hindi
Sunday	ytvar	ytvar, rəvivar
Monday	pir, or somvar	somvar
Tuesday	məngəl	məngəlvar
Wednesday	bwdh	bwdhvar
Thursday	jwmerat	bryhəspətivar, gwruvar
Friday	jwma	{wkrəvar
Saturday	sənicər, or həfta	{ənivar

jwmerat is the only one of these which is feminine. All the rest are masculine.

You'll find that there is some variation in usage. Many mother-tongue speakers of Urdu will not say 'somvar' for Monday, while Panjabis commonly will. Similarly, mother-tongue speakers will commonly say just 'məngəl', 'bwdh', while others will say 'məngəlvar', 'bwdhvar'. It's sensible to see what people say in your area, and to follow suit.

You'll also find that not all who speak and understand Urdu will use all of these words for the days. Even fluent speakers of Urdu will in many cases not use the Urdu names unless besides being Urdu speakers they are also Muslims. I explained in the Introduction, (p.5) that generally speaking no Hindu or Sikh will call Thursday and Friday jwmerat and jwma, because these names have reference to specifically Muslim observances. (The word jwma is related to one that means 'congregation' and indicates the day on which Muslims generally go to the mosque to pray together. The rat or jwmerat means 'night' and is here used in the same way as English uses 'eve' (e.g. 'Christmas eve') to indicate 'the day before'.) For this and other reasons South Asians in Britain will often use the English days of the week, especially in religiously-mixed company, since pretty well everyone understands them and they are, so to speak, religiously neutral. Older people will adapt them, as they adapt all English words they use, to the Urdu sound-system.

English translation of the dialogue - see if you can re-translate it into Urdu/Hindi.

10. A. Listen. Today's Friday. June, you tell [us], what day is [it] today?

11. J. Today's Friday.

12. A. [That]'s right. Today's Friday. Now listen: tomorrow will be hafta,[1] or sanicar.[1] [These are alternative names for Saturday.] Ann, you tell [us], tomorrow what day will it be?

13. Ann Tomorrow it will be hafta or sanicar.

14. A. Right. Tomorrow will be hafta - or sanicar. Now tell [us] - Ken, you tell us, the day after tomorrow what day will [it] be?

15. K. The day after tomorrow it will be Sunday.

16. A. Yes, and after that what day will it be? Margaret, you tell us.

17. M. After that it will be Monday.

18. A. Yes, it'll be Monday. And after that? Brian, you tell us.

19. B. After that it will be Tuesday.

20. A. And after Tuesday? Kate?

21. K. After Tuesday it will be Wednesday.

22. A. And after Wednesday? Tom?

23. T. After Wednesday it will be Thursday.

24. A. Yes, it'll be Thursday. Well done! And after that what day will it be? Terry?

25. T. After that it will be Friday.

26. A. Yes, and what day is it today? June?

27. J. Today's Friday.

28. A. And what day was it yesterday? Kate?

29. K. Yesterday was Thursday. And the day before yesterday was Wednesday, and before that it was Tuesday, and before that it was Monday, and before Monday it was Sunday, and before Sunday it was hafta,[1] or sanicar,[1] and before that it was Friday.

30. A. Very good! Well done!

_____

1. H. ʃanivar.

16.4 The future and past tenses of hona, 'to be'

Here is the complete future tense of hona

Feminine forms		Masculine forms*	
məyŋ huŋgi	I shall be	həyŋ huŋga	I shall be
[tu hogi]	[thou wilt be]	[tu hoga]	[thou wilt be]
yyh hogi	she[1,2] will be	yyh hoga	he[1,2] will be
vwh hogi	she[3,2] will be	vwh hoga	he[3,2] will be
həm hoŋge[4]	we shall be	həm hoŋge	we shall be
ap hoŋgi	you will be	ap hoŋge	you will be
twm hogi	you[2] will be	twm hoge	you[2] will be
yyh[5] hoŋgi	they[1] will be	yyh[5] hoŋge	they[1] will be
	she[1,7] will be		he[1,7] will be
vwh[6] hoŋgi	they[3] will be	vwh[6] hoŋge	they[3] will be
	she[3,7] will be		he[3,7] will be

And here is the complete past tense

Feminine forms		Masculine forms*	
məyŋ thi	I was	məyŋ tha	I was
[tu thi]	[thou wast]	[tu tha]	[thou wert]
yyh thi	she[1,2] was	yyh tha	he[1,2] was
vwh thi	she[3,2] was	vwh tha	he[3,2] was
həm the[8]	we were	həm the	we were
ap thiŋ	you were	ap the	you were
twm thiŋ	you[2] were	twm the	you[2] were
yyh[5] thiŋ	they[1] were	yyh[5] the	they[1] were
	she[1,7] was		he[1,7] was
vwh[6] thiŋ	they[3] were	vwh[6] the	they[3] were
	she[3,7] was		he[3,7] was

---

1. present.
2. junior status.
3. absent.
4. H., and many Panjabi speakers; hoŋgi.

5. H. ye.
6. H. ve.
7. ap status.
8. H., and many Panjabi speakers; thiŋ.

---

* The masculine plural forms are also used for mixed m. and f. subjects.

16.5 Practice

Practice asking and answering questions like these:

| kəl | ap | kəhaŋ | hoŋge/i | ? |
| | yyh[1] | | | |

| kəl | ap | kəhaŋ | the/thiŋ | ? |
| | yyh[1] | | | |

Notice that Muslims in answering any question about their (or others') future actions would nearly always use the words

ynʃah əllah
God willing

For Muslims who take their religion very seriously these words mean exactly what they imply. For others it would be fair to say that they say them for much the same reason as English people in similar circumstances say 'Touch wood!'. Anyway, they'll say them because they won't feel comfortable if they don't. Quite often they won't feel comfortable if you don't, and will add the words for you to any forecast you think fit to make.

---

1. H. plu. ye.

To follow unit 16

(The questions, except where otherwise indicated, are addressed to a woman.)

1. Q. kəl ap kytne bəje wt̪heŋgi?

2. W. kəl məyŋ ... bəje wt̪huŋgi.

3. Q. yyh[1] (indicating M) kytne bəje wt̪heŋge?   yn se puchiye.

4. W. (to the M) kəl ap kytne bəje wt̪heŋge?

5. M. məyŋ .... bəje wt̪huŋga.

6. W. yyh[1] .... bəje wt̪heŋge.

7. Q. ap naʃte meŋ kya khaeŋgi?

8. W. məyŋ .... əwr .... əwr .... khauŋgi.

9. Q. əwr kya pieŋgi?   cae?   kafi?   orənj jus?

10. W. məyŋ kafi piuŋgi.

11. Q. ap ghər se kytne bəje nykleŋgi?

12. W. məyŋ ghər se .... bəje nykluŋgi.

13. Q. ap am təwr pər[2] kytne bəje nykəlti həyŋ?

14. W. məyŋ am təwr pər .... bəje nykəlti huŋ.

15. Q. ap dopəhr ka khana kəhaŋ khaeŋgi?

16. W. .... meŋ khauŋgi.

17. Q. aj kya dyn həy?

18. A. aj .... həy.

19. Q. kəl kya dyn tha?

_____

1. H. ye.
2. am təwr pər - 'on general manner', generally.

20. A.   kəl .... tha.*

21. Q.   əwr pərsoŋ kya dyn tha?

22. A.   pərsoŋ .... tha.*

23. Q.   əwr ws se pəhle kya dyn tha?

24. A.   ws se pəhle .... tha.*

25. Q.   əwr ws se pəhle?

26. A.   ws se pəhle .... tha.*

27. Q.   swniye: kəl kya dyn hoga?

28. A.   kəl .... hoga.*

29. Q.   əwr pərsoŋ kya dyn hoga?

30. A.   pərsoŋ .... hoga.*

31. Q.   əwr ws ke bad?

32. A.   ws ke bad .... hoga.*

33. Q.   (to W) kəl ap kəhaŋ thiŋ?

34. W.   kəl məyŋ .... meŋ thi.

35. Q.   (to M) əwr ap? kəl ap kəhaŋ the?

36. M.   kəl məyŋ .... meŋ tha.

37. Q.   (to W) kəl ap kəhaŋ hoŋgi?

38. W.   kəl məyŋ .... meŋ huŋgi.

39. Q.   (to M) əwr ap? kəl ap kəhaŋ hoŋge?

40. M.   kəl məyŋ .... meŋ huŋga.

---

* tha/hoga will become thi, hogi in your answers whenever the day
is jwmerat.   All the other days are masculine.

171.

Unit 17. Times of day

This is a unit which you may well be studying on your own, since
there is nothing very complicated about it and if you are pressed for
time in class it may be sensible to move straight on to units 18 and
following.   To provide for this possibility I shall not assume in
units 18 and after that you have read this unit.   It is one that you
and/or your teachers can take up any time you/they think fit.

In unit 16 you learnt the days of the week.   Now that you know
them you can learn how to say what _time_ of day it is.

The divisions of the day are:

swbh (nearly always in Urdu, and always in Hindi,
pronounced swbəh - so in future I shall write it
like that) means 'morning'.

dopəhr means 'midday' - extending from about 12 to as long
as seems appropriate in any particular context.

tisra pəhr, or syhpəhr[1] means 'afternoon'.

ʃam means 'evening', but is quite often used where we in
English would say 'afternoon'.

rat means 'night'.

dyn, as you already know, means 'day'.

tisra pəhr (and syhpəhr) and dyn are masculine, and the rest are
feminine.

English uses a variety of prepositions with these words, while Urdu/
Hindi usually uses ko with all of them.

swbəh ko	in the morning
dopəhr ko	at midday
tisre pəhr ko	in the afternoon
syhpəhr[1] ko	
ʃam ko	in the evening (or, sometimes, in the afternoon)
rat ko	at night, by night
dyn ko	by day

---

1.   Only in Urdu.

Note that in Urdu/Hindi tonight is 'today night', <u>aj rat ko</u>.
Last night is 'yesterday night', <u>kəl rat ko</u>.

Note also:

<u>do dyn hue, do həfte hue, do məhine hue, do sal (bərəs)[1] hue</u>
Two days ago, two weeks ago, two months ago, two years ago.

  or

<u>do dyn pəhle</u> etc.
Two days ago etc.

You have met <u>həfta</u> as one of the two Urdu words for 'Saturday'.
Note that it also means 'week', in both Urdu and Hindi.

<u>ys həfte</u>, <u>ys məhine</u>, <u>ys sal (bərəs)[1]</u>   )
this week, this month, this year   )
)
<u>əgle həfte</u>, <u>əgle məhine</u>, <u>əgle sal (bərəs)</u>) (as adverbs)
next week, next month, next year   )
)
<u>pychle həfte</u>, <u>pychle məhine</u>, <u>pychle sal (bərəs)</u>)
last week, last month, last year   )

You tell the time by using a verb that really means 'to ring, to
sound, to strike'. 'What's the time?' is expressed as:

<u>ys   vəqt[2] kytne bəje həyŋ?</u>
[at] this time how many have struck?

  or

<u>kya bəja həy?</u>
What has struck?

You learnt the word <u>bəje</u> ad hoc in the sense of '[at]....o'clock'
in unit 9. You also learnt some of the ways of expressing 'a quarter
to', 'a quarter past' and 'half past'. There are other special words
that occur in the range of times from 12.45 to 2.30. Here is a list
of the times from a quarter to one to a half past three which will
illustrate them:

<u>pəwn bəja həy</u>
One-less-a-quarter has struck
i.e. It's a quarter to one

<u>ek bəja həy</u>
One has struck
i.e. It's one o'clock

---

1. H. also, but less commonly, vərʃ.
2. H. also, and more commonly, səməy.

<u>səva bəja həy</u>
1¼ has struck
i.e. It's a quarter past one

<u>derh bəja həy</u>
1½ has struck
i.e. It's half past one

Watch the pronunciation of this - ḍ and ṛ both retroflex, and the ṛ <u>also</u> aspirated.

<u>pəwne do bəje həyŋ</u>
'Two-less-a-quarter have struck'
i.e. It's a quarter to two.

Note that it's not until you get to a quarter to two that you start using the plural verb.   <u>derh</u> - one and a half - still has a singular - <u>bəja həy</u>.

Then:　　　<u>do bəje həyŋ</u>
Two have struck
i.e. It's two o'clock

<u>səva do bəje həyŋ</u>
2¼ have struck
i.e. It's a quarter past two

<u>ḍhai bəje həyŋ</u>
2½ have struck
i.e. It's half past two

Watch the pronunciation - ḍ retroflex, <u>and</u> aspirated.

<u>pəwne tin bəje həyŋ</u>
'Three less a quarter have struck'
i.e. It's a quarter to three

<u>tin bəje həyŋ</u>
It's three o'clock

<u>səva tin bəje həyŋ</u>
3¼　　　have struck
It's a quarter past three

<u>saṛhe tin bəje həyŋ</u>
3½　　　have struck
It's half past three

From a quarter to three onwards the pattern is quite regular.

pəwne tin, 1/4 to 3	pəwne car, 1/4 to 4	pəwne panc.... 1/4 to 5....
səva tin, 3 1/4	səva car, 4 1/4	səva panc.... 5 1/4....
saṛhe tin, 3 1/2	saṛhe car, 4 1/2	saṛhe panc.... 5 1/2

But don't forget the slightly different words that are used for the quarter-hours and half-hours from a quarter to one to half past two.

Now you'll need to know how to say (e.g.)

      It's twenty-five to four

and

      It's ten past five

For the present we will work in five-minute units. The words for 'five' and 'ten' you already know. 'Fifteen' you don't need.

      'Twenty' is <u>bis</u>

      'Twenty-five' is <u>pəccis</u>   (Note the double 'c'.)

For minutes <u>to</u> the hour you say the equivalent of (e.g.):

      'In one (two, three...) striking 25 (20, 10, 5) minutes are'

      <u>ek (do, tin...) bəjne men pəccis (bis, dəs, panc) mynət həyn.</u>

      i.e., It's 25 (20, 10, 5) minutes to 1 (2, 3).

Note the pronunciation of <u>mynət</u>.

For minutes <u>past</u> the hour you say the equivalent of (e.g.):

      'One (two, three...) having-struck, 25 (20, 10, 5) minutes are'

      <u>ek (do, tin...) bəjkər pəccis (bis, dəs, panc) mynət həyn.</u>

      i.e., It's 25 (20, 10, 5) minutes past 1 (2, 3).

'bəjkər' means 'having struck'. (You can also say '<u>bəjke</u>' instead of '<u>bəjkər</u>'. Either is O.K.)

To tell the time <u>exactly</u> you will need to know all the numbers up to 29. (But you can get by if you tell it to the nearest five minutes!) And to state the date you need 30 and 31 as well. I give the numbers 1 to 31 as an appendix, and with them a note about dates.

If you want to practice time-telling in pairs you don't need a clock-face. You can ask:

<u>tin mynət pəhle kytne bəje the</u>?
'Three minutes ago how many had struck?'
i.e. What time was it three minutes ago?

<u>or</u>

<u>do mynət ke bad kytne bəje honge</u>?
'After two minutes how many will have struck?'
i.e. What time will it be in two minutes' time?

Note that

     <u>At</u> one o'clock   is   <u>ek bəje</u> (without any postposition)

while

     <u>At</u> 20 to 2   is   do bəjne men bis mynət <u>pər</u>

The rule is that the hours and the half-hours and quarter-hours
have <u>no</u> postposition.   Other times have -<u>pər</u>.

     <u>tren sərhe tin bəje jati həy</u>
The train goes at half-past three

But

     <u>tren tin bəjkər</u> (or, <u>bəjke</u>) <u>pəccis mynət pər jati həy</u>
The train goes at twenty-five past three.

Unit 18.   What you did yesterday

18.1   Daily routine in the simple past

In earlier units you've talked about daily routines, first in
the present, and later in the future.   Now we're going to talk about them
in the simple past - i.e. you're going to say 'Today I got up at 7 o'clock.
I had tea', etc.

Listen to, and read, these sentences.   You'll understand the meaning
alright, even if you don't <u>quite</u> understand how they work; and the picture
on the page facing this one will help you.   The first vertical column
shows what <u>I</u> did, and the second what my wife/həsina did.   But you'll also
notice some unexpected things which, later, we'll go on to discuss.

1.   aj məyŋ sat bəje wʈha.

2.   bivi[1] aʈh bəje wʈhiŋ.

3.   pəhle məyŋ ne cae pi.

4.   bivi[1] ne bhi cae pi.

5.   ws ke bad həm ne naʃta kiya.

6.   naʃte meŋ məyŋ ne do tos khae əwr do ənɖe khae.

7.   bivi[1] ne syrf ek tos khaya əwr ek ənɖa khaya.

8.   phyr məyŋ ne kafi pi.

9.   bivi[1] ne dudh piya.

10.   nəw bəje məyŋ ghər se nykla əwr dəftər gəya.

11.   məyŋ ne <u>həsina</u> ke sath dopəhr ka khana khaya.

12.   pəhle məyŋ ne orənj jus piya.

13.   <u>həsina</u> ne orənj jus nəhiŋ piya.

14.   phyr məyŋ ne goʃt[2] khaya.

15.   <u>həsina</u> ne amleʈ khaya.

16.   məyŋ ne goʃt[2] ke sath səbziyəŋ khaiŋ.

17.   phyr həm donoŋ ne rəsməlai khai əwr kafi pi.

---

1.   H. pətni.
2.   H. or, but less commonly, mas.

English translation

(Notes follow this translation.   If there's anything that you don't
follow and they don't explain, look back to p. 90.   You should find
the explanation there.)

1.   Today I got up at 7 o'clock.

2.   [My] wife got up at 8 o'clock.

3.   First I drank tea.

4.   [My] wife also drank tea.

5.   After that we had breakfast.

6.   I had two eggs and two slices of toast for breakfast.

7.   My wife had only one piece of toast and one egg.

8.   Then I drank coffee.

9.   My wife drank milk.

10. At 9 o'clock I left the house and went to the office.

11. I had lunch with Hasina.

12. First I drank orange juice.

13. Hasina didn't drink orange juice.

14. Then I ate meat.

15. Hasina ate an omelette.

16. I ate vegetables with the meat.

17. Then we both ate rasmalai and drank coffee.

Notes

First, one or two things you need to know about the vocabulary. You know that the standard way of forming the past participle is to add a to the root.

rəh

rəha, i, e

You also know that when a root ends in a vowel, you stick a y in between the root and the a ending.

ana		to come
a		
a-y-a		

(But not the -i and -e endings — ai and ae, aiŋ are the correct forms.)

You also know that some verbs have irregular past participles

	jana	to go
Root:	ja	
	gəya, gəi, gəe, gəiŋ	went

In these sentences you have:

	pina	to drink
past ppl.	piya, pi, pie, piŋ	
	kərna	to do, to make
past ppl.	kiya, ki, kie, kiŋ	
	khana	to eat
past ppl.	khaya, khai, khae, khaiŋ	

Now let's see what you notice about these sentences - or some of them - which strike you as odd.   Take them one by one, and write down the answer to the question, Is there anything odd?   Answers 1 to 4 should be:

1.   No.

2.   No.

3.   Yes, the word ne after məyŋ.   The subject of the sentence is "I" (a man) so you would expect a masculine singular form of the verb; instead the verb has a feminine singular form.

4.   Yes, the word ne after bivi.[1]   With "bivi" as the subject of the sentence you would expect a courteous plural verb form;   instead the verb is in the feminine singular form.

I list the other answers on the next page.   Don't look at them until you've worked out your own!

1.1 H. pətni.

5. Yes, the word <u>ne</u> after <u>həm</u>.   Subj. m. (or, rather mixed) plu.
    Vb. m. sg.

6. Yes, the word <u>ne</u> after <u>məyŋ</u>.   Subj. m. sg.   Vbs. m. plu.

7. Yes, the word <u>ne</u> after <u>bivi</u>.   Subj. f., calling for a courteous
    f. plu. vb.   Vbs. m. sg.

8. Yes, the word <u>ne</u> after <u>məyŋ</u>.   Subj. m. sg.   Vb. f. sg.

9. Yes, the word <u>ne</u> after <u>bivi</u>.   Subj. f. calling for a courteous
    f. plu. vb.   Vb. m. sg.

10. No.

11. Yes, the word <u>ne</u> after <u>məyŋ</u>.

12. Yes, the word <u>ne</u> after <u>məyŋ</u>.

13. Yes, the word <u>ne</u> after <u>həsina</u>.   Subj. f. calling for a courteous
    f. plu. vb.   Vb. m. sg.

14. Yes, the word <u>ne</u> after <u>məyŋ</u>.

15. Yes, the word <u>ne</u> after <u>həsina</u>.   Subj. f. calling for a courteous
    f. plu. vb.   Vb. m. sg.

16. Yes, the word <u>ne</u> after <u>məyŋ</u>.   Subj. m. sg.   Vb. f. plu.

17. Yes, the word <u>ne</u> after <u>həm donoŋ</u>.   Subj. mixed plu.   Vbs. f. sg.

So the first and most obvious thing that is common to all the 'odd' sentences is that the word <u>ne</u> follows the subject.

What's common to sentences 3, 4, 5, 6, 7, 8, 9, 13, 15, 16 and 17?

First, that the verbs don't agree with their subjects.

Can you see what, in every case, they <u>do</u> agree with?

If you look carefully you'll see that in every case they agree with their objects. And actually this is true also of sentences 11, 12 and 14. It just so happens that the subjects have the same number and gender as the verbs, but so do the objects, and it's the objects that the verbs agree with.

So what's the explanation of all this? It's a fairly long one, but not too difficult. Let's begin by looking again at some of the past tenses you've already met. Among them are two tenses formed with the past participle.

Two of the tenses formed with the past participle - the simple past
and the perfect - you have already met.

> məyŋ paŋc sal vəhaŋ <u>rəha</u>
> I <u>lived</u> there five years

> məyŋ wmər bhər vəhaŋ <u>rəha huŋ</u>
> I <u>have lived</u> there all my life

Two other tenses are formed with the past participle. I give them
the usual labels, but it doesn't matter much whether you remember them
or not. All you <u>need</u> to remember is the equivalent English tense.

| The pluperfect | məyŋ vəhaŋ rəha tha (f. rəhi thi) |
| means | I had lived there |

The future perfect	məyŋ vəhaŋ rəha huŋga (f. rəhi huŋgi)
means	I will have lived there
or	I must have lived there

You need to know these tenses in order to understand one very
important thing about the Urdu/Hindi verb system. And this involves
the use of two words - transitive and intransitive. You need to know
the difference between transitive and intransitive verbs because in
those tenses formed with the past participle - the ones we've just
set out - transitive verbs behave quite differently from intransitive
verbs.

Some of you may not be too sure of the meanings of 'intransitive'
and 'transitive', and moreover different people use the words in slightly
different ways. So let me explain how I use the words in this course.
In this course I shall use transitive to mean a verb of which you can
ask 'Whom?' or 'What?'.

> e.g. <u>dekhna</u>, to see; <u>swnna</u>, to hear; <u>kəhna</u>, to say - all
> these are transitive verbs, since you may ask, To see
> whom? To hear what? etc. - while <u>jana</u>, to go; <u>ana</u>, to
> come; <u>sona</u>, to sleep, etc., are <u>not</u> transitive verbs -
> i.e. are <u>in</u>transitive verbs.

In English, a good many verbs have transitive and intransitive forms
which are identical. e.g. In

> Term <u>began</u> on October 5th

'began' is intransitive. But in

> He <u>began</u> work on October 10th

'began' is transitive.

In Urdu/Hindi transitive and intransitive forms are rarely identical. Thus 'to begin' (intr.) is ʃwru hona, and 'to begin' (tr.) is ʃwru kərna. 'To burn' (intr.) is jəlna, and 'to burn' (tr.) is jəlana.

The first thing you have to learn is that in those tenses formed with the past participle only <u>intransitive</u> verbs behave as you would expect, with the verb agreeing with the subject in gender and number.

> vwh ləndən meŋ rəha.
> He lived in London.

> yyh ləndən meŋ rəhi həy.
> She has lived in London.

> həm ləndən meŋ rəhe the. (H., and many Panjabi speakers,
> of Urdu f. rəhi thiŋ)
>
> We had lived in London.

> vwh ləndən meŋ rəhe hoŋge.
> They (m. or mixed) will have (or, must have) lived in
> London.

> vwh ləndən meŋ rəhi hoŋgi.
> They (f.) will have (or, must have) lived in London.

<u>Transitive</u> verbs behave quite differently in these tenses. The first difference is that the subject is followed by the word <u>ne</u>, and the verb agrees <u>not</u> with the subject but with the <u>object</u>.

Now let's go back to the sentences about having got up, had tea, and so on, and see how they illustrate this rule. Take them one by one and answer the questions about them like this:

Sentence 1.   Why no <u>ne</u>?   vb. is intransitive.

2.   Why no <u>ne</u>?   vb. is intransitive.

3, 4.   Why <u>ne</u>?   Because the vb. is transitive.

Why <u>pi</u>?   Agreeing with object <u>cae</u>, which is f.

The answers for the rest of the 17 sentences are on the next page. Go through them, making sure you understand why each sentence has the form it has. Then listen to the sentences once again, reading as you do so. Now use the picture cues on p.176 and try to say the sentence about each picture without looking at the text - then check in the text to see if you are right. When you can do this, try to work out the <u>questions</u> you'd ask to elicit these 17 sentences as replies.

5. <u>ne</u> because the verb (<u>kərna</u>) is transitive.

   <u>kiya</u> agreeing with the object (<u>naʃta</u>), which is m. sg.

6. <u>ne</u> because the verb (<u>khana</u>) is transitive.

   <u>khae</u> (in both cases) agreeing with the object (in both cases) which is m. plu.

7. <u>ne</u> because the verb (<u>khana</u>) is transitive.

   <u>khaya</u> (in both cases) agreeing with the object (in both cases) which is m. sg.

8. <u>ne</u> because the verb (<u>pina</u>) is transitive.

   <u>pi</u> agreeing with the object (<u>kafi</u>), which is f. sg.

9. <u>ne</u> because the verb (<u>pina</u>) is transitive.

   <u>piya</u> agreeing with the object (<u>dudh</u>), which is m. sg.

10. No <u>ne</u> because the verbs are intransitive.

11. <u>ne</u> because the verb (<u>khana</u>) is transitive.

    <u>khaya</u> agreeing with the object <u>khana</u>, which is m. sg.

12. <u>ne</u> because the verb (<u>pina</u>) is transitive.

    <u>piya</u> agreeing with the object (<u>orənj jus</u>), which is m. sg.

13. As for 12.

14. <u>ne</u> because the verb (<u>khana</u>) is transitive.

    <u>khaya</u> agreeing with the object (<u>goʃt</u>) which is m. sg.

15. <u>ne</u> because the verb (<u>khana</u>) is transitive.

    <u>khaya</u> agreeing with the object (<u>amleṭ</u>), which is m. sg.

16. <u>ne</u> because the verb (<u>khana</u>) is transitive.

    <u>khaiŋ</u> agreeing with the object (<u>səbziyaŋ</u>), which is f. plu.

17. <u>ne</u> because the verbs (<u>khana, pina</u>) are transitive.

    <u>khai</u>, <u>pi</u> agreeing with their respective objects, which are f. sg.

To follow unit 18, section 1

(All questions are addressed to a woman.)

1. Q. aj ap kytne bəje wţhiŋ?

2. W. aj məyŋ .... bəje wţhi.

3. Q. ap ne naʃte meŋ kya khaya?

4. W. məyŋ ne .... əwr .... khaya/khae/khaiŋ.

5. Q. ap [dəftər, skul, ...] kytne bəje pəhwŋciŋ?

6. W. məyŋ .... bəje pəhwŋci.

7. Q. ap ne dopəhr ka khana kəhaŋ khaya?

8. W. məyŋ ne dopəhr ka khana .... meŋ khaya.

9. Q. ap ghər kytne bəje vapəs aiŋ?

10. W. məyŋ ghər .... bəje vapəs ai.

11. Q. ap ne rat ka khana kysi ke sath khaya?

12. W. ji nəhiŋ, kysi ke sath nəhiŋ khaya.

    or

    ji haŋ, məyŋ ne rat ka khana .... ke sath khaya.

13. Q. ap kytne bəje soiŋ?

14. W. məyŋ .... bəje soi.

18.2 <u>əllah ek həy</u>

Now listen to, and read, this short passage - simplified a bit from the original - about God the Creator.   It's taken from a booklet written to teach Muslim children the basic beliefs of Islam, and includes quite a lot of words you've never met.   I'll list them under the passage in the order in which they occur.[1]

Listen to the passage repeatedly until you no longer have to look at the word list - in other words, until you can understand everything as you hear it.

This is the first time you've been asked to do this.   The object of the course has been to help you to learn all the basic structures of the language as quickly as possible without being confronted with the additional task of learning a lot of vocabulary.   Once you have finished this and the next three units, your next need will be to expand considerably the range of your vocabulary, and I wrote Part III, with Part II as a reference book geared to it,[2] to help you meet that need. If from the start you've been using such Urdu as you know in conversation with Urdu/Hindi speakers - and that's what you <u>should</u> have been doing - you will have repeatedly been in the situation of hearing <u>some</u> words and expressions you don't understand, but nevertheless picking up the general sense.   Some of the dialogue exercises I have given you in earlier lessons were designed to get you to feel relaxed about doing this - and you should <u>still</u> feel relaxed when you meet a passage like this one, taking in what you can, going to the notes for help, listening and reading again, and repeating these processes until you understand <u>everything</u>.

So henceforth I shall not be restricting to the same extent as hitherto the range of vocabulary which the passages use.

əllah ne sara jəhan bənaya - zəmin bənai əwr asman

bənaya;   sytare bənae əwr surəj əwr cand;   səməndər[3]

bənae əwr dərya əwr pəhaɽ.   əllah ne həm ko aŋkheŋ diŋ,

kan diye, əwr dyl diye.

sara	all, the whole
jəhan	world
bənana	to make
zəmin	earth
asman	the sky

---

1.   This is an Urdu passage.   Non-Muslims don't use the word Allah for God.   I'll be giving the full passage, with notes on Hindi equivalents, later (on pp. 194-5).

2.   Perhaps I ought to have called Part III Part II, and vice versa.

3.   Some speakers pronounce this <u>səmwndər</u>.

sytara	star
surəj	sun
cand	moon
səməndər, səmwndər	sea
dərya	river
pəhaɾ	mountain
aɳkh	eye
dena	to give. (Its past participle forms are slightly irregular.)
kan	ear
dyl	heart, mind

The passage means:

> Allah (God) made the whole world. [He] made the earth
> and [He] made the sky; [He] made the stars and the sun
> and the moon; [He] made the seas and the rivers and the
> mountains. Allah gave to us eyes, [He] gave [us] ears,
> [He] gave [us] hearts.

Now take the first sentence of the passage, and work out why the verb is sometimes <u>bənaya</u>, sometimes <u>bənai</u>, and sometimes <u>bənae</u>.

Answers upside down at the bottom of the page.[1]

Now list the vocabulary as far as you can in a way which <u>shows</u> you the gender of the words. There are four about which you can't tell the gender. Which are they? Answers at the bottom of the page.[2]

The plural of <u>dərya</u> is also <u>dərya</u> - it's one of the few masculines in -<u>a</u> that don't change to -<u>e</u> for the plural.

<u>diya</u>, <u>di</u>, <u>diye</u>, <u>diɳ</u>

is the slightly irregular past participle of <u>dena</u>.

---

1. <u>bənaya</u> - m.sg. agreeing with m.sg. obj. jəhan. <u>banai</u> agreeing with f.sg. object zəmin. <u>bənaya</u> - m.sg. agreeing with m.sg. obj. asman. <u>bənae</u> - m.plu. agreeing with m.plu. sytare. <u>bənae</u> - obj. agreeing with m.plu. səməndər.

2. surəj, cand, dərya, and pəhaɾ. They're all in fact masculine.

There are only four common verbs, including <u>dena</u>, which have past participles on this pattern:

pina to drink		piya, pi, piye, piŋ
lena to take	with past participles	liya, li, liye, liŋ
dena to give		diya, di, diye, diŋ
kərna to do, make		kiya, ki, kiye, kiŋ

Unit 19.   What did she say?

Listen to, and read, the following short dialogue:

1.   Bashir: <u>Alison</u>, aj ap kytne bəje wʈhiŋ?

2.   Alison: aj məyŋ aʈh bəje wʈhi.

3.   Bashir: <u>Farida</u>, məyŋ ne <u>Alison</u> se kya pucha?

4.   Farida: ap ne <u>Alison</u> se pucha ky 'aj ap kytne bəje wʈhiŋ?'

5.   Bashir: əwr <u>Alison</u> ne kya kəha?

6.   Farida: <u>Alison</u> ne kəha ky 'aj məyŋ aʈh bəje wʈhi'.

What do you notice about it?

There are two things: the word <u>ky</u>, and the verb in the masculine singular before it

        ap ne <u>Alison</u> se puch<u>a</u> ky...

and

   <u>Alison</u> ne kəh<u>a</u> ky...

<u>kəha</u> is the past participle of <u>kəhna</u>, 'to say'.

You'll have guessed the meaning.   Now see how the dialogue would look in natural English translation:

1.   B.   Alison, what time did you get up today?

2.   A.   I got up at eight o'clock today.

3.   B.   Farida, what did I ask Alison?

4.   F.   You asked Alison what time she got up.

5.   B.   And what did Alison say?

6.   F.   Alison said she got up at 8 o'clock.

In English, sentences like 4 and 6 are described as being examples of 'indirect speech'.   In Urdu/Hindi, strictly speaking, there is no indirect speech.   You can regard the ky as the equivalent of inverted commas, and what follows it are the actual words that the speaker said - his/her 'direct speech'.

(This is a general rule.   I shall note exceptions as they occur.)

If you translate into natural English, then the ky will correspond to English 'that', but while in English you can often omit the 'that' (as in sentences 4 and 6) in Urdu/Hindi you can never omit the ky: moreover you have the ky even where you couldn't have the 'that' in English.   (Compare the Urdu/Hindi and English versions of sentence 4).

So, to put it briefly, the first point to note is that there is no indirect speech in Urdu/Hindi.   Reported speech is introduced by ky, and the speaker's actual words follow.

The second point to note is that the verb before the ky always ends in -a — in other words the sentence or sentences following ky are the object of the sentence, and are regarded as a masculine singular.

If you are learning in class, you can now practise this - with your teachers and with one another - like this:

A.   Jean, aj ap kytne bəje wṭhiŋ?

Jean   aj mayŋ sat bəje wṭhi.

A.   John, mayŋ ne Jean se kya pucha?

John   ap ne pucha ky 'aj ap kytne bəje wṭhiŋ?'

A.   əwr Jean ne kya kəha?

John   Jean ne kəha ky 'aj mayŋ sat bəje wṭhi'.

and so on, right through the daily routine.   Another way to practise this - on your own or with a partner - is to listen to any of the earlier dialogues in the course, and stop the cassette after each couple of sentences to report what was said.   Eg. From unit 4,

Sentence 28:   Alison: - ap Oxford meŋ kəhaŋ rəhti həyŋ?

          29:   June: - mayŋ Cowley meŋ rəhti huŋ.

          Alison ne pucha ky 'ap Oxford meŋ kəhaŋ rəhti həyŋ?'
          əwr June ne kəha ky 'mayŋ Cowley meŋ rəhti huŋ.'

To follow unit 19

(All questions are addressed to a woman.)

1. Q. aj ap kytne bəje wʈhiŋ?

2. W. aj məyŋ .... bəje wʈhi.

3. Q. məyŋ ne ap se kya pucha?

4. W. ap ne mwjh se pucha ky 'aj ap kytne bəje wʈhiŋ?'

5. Q. əwr ap ne kya kəha?

6. W. məyŋ ne kəha ky 'aj məyŋ .... bəje wʈhi'.

7. Q. aj ap ne naʃta kiya?

8. W. ji haŋ, ⌊məyŋ ne⌋ naʃta kiya.

9. Q. məyŋ ne ap se kya pucha?

10. W. ap ne mwjh se pucha ky 'aj ap ne naʃta kiya?'

11. Q. əwr ap ne kya kəha?

12. A. məyŋ ne kəha ky 'ji haŋ, naʃta kiya'.

13. Q. ap am təwr pər kytne bəje [dəftər, skul ....] jati həyŋ?

14. W. məyŋ am təwr pər .... bəje .... jati huŋ.

15. Q. məyŋ ne ap se kya pucha?

16. W. ap ne mwjh se pucha ky 'ap am təwr pər kytne bəje ....
jati həyŋ.'

17. Q. əwr ap ne kya kəha?

18. W. məyŋ ne kəha ky 'am təwr pər məyŋ .... bəje .... jati huŋ.'

Unit 20.   A school evening.

Now listen to, and read, this short passage.   It's about a parent going to attend a performance at her children's school.   It's a continuous passage, but I've written the sentences separately and numbered them so that you can easily refer back to them.   There are one or two new constructions that you won't understand.   The words that are probably new to you are listed and explained after the passage.

1.   məyŋ vəqt[1] se zəra pəhle pəhwŋci əwr hal meŋ gəi.

2.   məyŋ ne dekha ky tin lərkiyəŋ əwr do ləɽke ʂtej pər program[2] ki təyyariyəŋ kər rəhe həyŋ.

3.   wnhoŋ ne mwjhe nəhiŋ dekha.

4.   məyŋ ʂtej ke pas bəyʈh gəi.

5.   bəccoŋ ko ɣəwr se dekha əwr...

6.   ....məhsus[3] kiya ky tinoŋ lərkiyoŋ ko məyŋ ne pəhle bhi dekha həy...

7.   məgər ləɽkoŋ meŋ se məyŋ ne syrf ek ko pəhle dekha həy.

8.   əb dusre ləɽke ne mwjhe dekha...

9.   ...əwr mwskərake 'helo' kəha.

Notes

...se zəra pəhle	a little before
pəhwŋcna	to arrive
hal	hall
ʂtej	stage
təyyari	preparation
wnhoŋ	(to be explained later!)
bəyʈh jana	to sit down
ɣəwr	attention, concentration
ɣəwr se	attentively
məhsus[3] kərna	to feel, notice, realise

---

1.   H. səməy.
2.   H. karyəkrəm.
3.   H. ənwbhəv.

tinoŋ	all three
məgər	but
syrf	only
dusra	second, other
mwskərake	smilingly, with a smile

Translation

1. I arrived a little before time and went into the hall.

2. I saw that 'three girls and two boys on the stage are making preparations of (i.e. for) the programme'.

3. They didn't see me.

4. I sat down near the stage.

5. [I] looked at the children attentively and...

6. ....realised that 'All three girls I have seen before too...

7. ...but out of the boys I've seen only one before.'

8. Now the second (or, other) boy looked in my direction...

9. ...and smilingly said 'Hello'.

   Notice that, as sentences 2 and 6 show, 'indirect speech' is a sort of catch-all phrase, because it isn't always, strictly speaking, 'speech' that is being reported.

Now look at the passage again and see if you can work out the answers to these questions.   Answers upside down at the bottom of the page.

Sentence 1.   pəhwŋci - what does this tell you?   Is the 'parent' a mother or a father?[1]

Why no ne?[2]

Sentence 2.   məyŋ ne dekha - why dekha?[3]

Why kər rəhe həyŋ?[4]

Sentence 3.   'wnhoŋ ne mwjhe nəhiŋ dekha'.   You know what it means.   But why wnhoŋ?[5]   And why dekha?[5] (You know that the mwjhe refers to a woman.)[5]

Sentence 5.   Why 'dekha?[5]   (The object is mixed m. and f.)

Sentence 6.   Why 'dekha həy'?[5]   (The object is f. plu.)

Sentence 8.   Why 'dusre ləɾke ne'?[5]

Look at the 'odd' sentences:

3.   wnhoŋ ne mwjhe nəhiŋ dekha.

5.   bəccoŋ ko ɣəwr se dekha...

6.   ...lərkiyoŋ ko məyŋ ne...dekha həy.

8.   ...dusre ləɾke ne mwjhe dekha.

First look at the verbs.   What do they all have in common?

All are in the masc. sing. form, regardless of the object.

Now look at the objects.   What do they have in common?

All are expressed with ko - or the equivalent;   mwjhe - mwjh ko.

---

5. You don't know!   I'm about to tell you.
4. Because it's the tense of the direct speech.
3. Because the object is a whole sentence.
2. Because pəhwŋcna is not a transitive verb.
1. Mother - pəhwŋci ends in -i.

Now look at the subjects in sentences 3 and 5.

In 3 <u>wnhoŋ ne</u> - means 'they'.

Before <u>ne</u> vwh plu. becomes <u>wnhoŋ</u>.

In 8 <u>dusre laᵣke ne</u>... means 'the other boy'.

These sentences illustrate (in part) new rules you need to know:

1. Before <u>ne</u>, while all except the 3rd person pronouns remain unchanged, these change their form as follows:

<u>yyh</u> sg.	becomes	ys
<u>vwh</u> sg.	"	ws
<u>yyh</u>[1] plu.	"	ynhoŋ
<u>vwh</u>[2] plu.	"	wnhoŋ

2. Before <u>ne</u>, nouns take their oblique form.

3. When the object is expressed with <u>ko</u> (or the equivalent - e.g. <u>mwjhe</u>, <u>həmeŋ</u>, <u>yse</u>, etc.) the form of the verb is invariably masc. sing.

20.2   əllah ek həy

Now let's look at another example of this rule operating. Earlier* you read a passage about Allah.   At that stage I modified the actual original to illustrate the agreement-of-verb-with-object rule.   Now look at the actual original.   In this text I've given Hindi equivalents in brackets.   Sikhs, and many Hindus, are, like Muslims, monotheist, but only Muslims use the word <u>əllah</u> for God.   <u>bhəgvan</u> is an acceptable word for God to Sikhs and Hindus alike.   With this substitution, the passage would be acceptable to them, but a Hindu writer would not be likely to write a passage of this kind.   (Here the numbers above the words refer to the notes that follow.)

əllah (bhəgvan) ek həy.[1]   ws ka koi ʃərik[2] nəhiŋ.   vwh həmeʃa[3] se həy əwr həmeʃa rəhega.   ws ne sare jəhan (səŋsar)[4] ko bənaya;[5] zəmin (dhərti)[6] ko bənaya əwr asman (also, and more commonly, akaʃ)[7] ko bənaya.   sytare[8] bənae əwr surəj[9] əwr

---

1. H. ye.
2. H. ve.

* In Unit 18.

cand (or, but less common candra, or candrama).[10] samandar
(or, more commonly, samwdra)[11] banae awr darya (nadiyaŋ)[12]
awr pahaṛ.[13]

ws ne ham ko aŋkheŋ[14] diŋ,[15] ky[16] dekheŋ;[17] kan[18] diye,
ky swneŋ; dyl (or, more commonly, man)[19] diye, ky soceŋ...[20]

Notes

1. God is one – the central belief of all Muslims.

2. ʃarik – sharer, partner.

        'His any partner not' – i.e. He has no partner.

    In Islam, the view that any other shares in the powers that
    belong to God alone is the gravest heresy. ʃarik is a purely
    Urdu word. The nearest H. would be 'sathi', companion, which
    is also good Urdu.

3. always

        'He is from always and will always remain'

4. world – How can you tell that it's masculine?[1] (Answers to this
    and later questions, upside down at the bottom of the page.)

5. banana – to make.

    why ne?[2]

    Why 'sare'?[3]

    Why 'banaya'?[4]

6. zamin (dharti) – fem. (though you can't tell this from the context) =
    earth, land.

7. asman (akaʃ) – masc. (though you can't tell this from the context) –
    sky.

8. sytara – star

    Why banae?[5]

---

5. agreeing with the object sytare.
4. because the object is expressed with ko.
3. Because jahan is a masculine noun in the oblique, as you can tell by the
    postposition ko which follows it. The adjective sara therefore goes
    into the oblique in agreement.
2. because banana is transitive.
1. from the masc. form sara of the adjective agreeing with it.

9. sun (m.).

10. moon (m.).

11. səməndər (səmwdra) (m.) _ sea. Here, does it mean 'sea', or 'seas'?[1]

12. dərya (m.) _ river. Here it means river__s__. dərya is one of a small group of masculines ending in _a which behave like masculines __not__ ending in _a.

> dərya _ river
>
> dərya men _ in the river
>
> dərya _ rivers
>
> dəryaon men _ in the rivers

(nədi is, of course, f., and declines like other feminines in _i.)

13. pəhaɾ _ mountain, hill.

14. aŋkh _ eye.

15. diŋ _ f.plu. of past participle of dena, agreeing with the f.plu. aŋkheŋ.

16. ky _ that; here in the sense of 'in order that'.

17. subjunctive _ 'we may see'.

18. kan _ ear. The diye (m.plu.) shows that kan here is plural, cf. note 11.

19. dyl (mən) _ heart. But here, as often, in the sense of 'mind'.

20. socna _ to think, reflect.

A question that is probably occurring to all of you is, 'When do you, and when don't you, express the object with ko?' The answer is that you can't give more than very general guidance _ and I gave it at the **top of page 156**. If you look at the passage we've just read you'll see that the only reason why the writer switches from object without ko to object with ko and back again seems to be that the passage would be very monotonous if he didn't.

---

1. It means 'seas'. How can you tell? Because it is the object, and the verb pənse agrees with it. pənse is a m.plu. form. Therefore səməndər must be m.plu.

Translation

God is one. He has no partner. He is from always and will
always remain. He made the whole world; [He] made the earth and
[He] made the sky. [He] made the stars and sun and moon. [He]
made the seas and rivers and mountains. He gave to us eyes that
[we] may see, gave [us] ears that [we] may hear, gave [us] hearts
(here = minds) that [we] may think...

Unit 21.   Visiting Qudsia

21.1   More on transitives: complete rules

Now that you have grasped the difference between transitives and intransitives, and seen, with a good many examples, how this affects the behaviour of the simple past, let me give you a complete set of rules about them.   Don't be daunted by their complexity! I'll say something about that in a minute.   Here are the rules:

1.   Tenses which may be called the simple past, perfect, pluperfect and future perfect (I said, I have said, I had said, I will have said[1]) are formed from the past participle.

2.   Some past participles are irregular:

Roots ending in a vowel regularly insert y before the -a

ending of the m. sing. form of the past participle.

jana has past participle gəya.

(Compound verbs of which the last element is jana follow suit. e.g. lejana has participle legəya.)

Common transitive verbs with irregular past participles are:

		m. sing.	f. sing.	m. plu.	f. plu.
dena,	to give	diya	di	diye	diŋ
lena,	to take to receive	liya	li	liye	liŋ
kərna,	to do to make	kiya	ki	kiye	kiŋ

3.   Most transitive verbs take ne in these tenses, but there are some common exceptions:

lana, le ana	to bring
lejana	to take away

and, in most contexts,

bolna	to speak
səməjhna[2]	to understand

---

1.   Often in the sense of 'must have said'.
2.   You met ap səmjhe?/səmjhiŋ? explained ad hoc in unit 10 (p. 106). Note also how it illustrates the rule given with reference to nykəlna in unit 16 (p. 162).

4. Before <u>ne</u> nouns take their oblique form.   Pronouns mostly
    remain unchanged, but

yyh (sing.)	becomes	ys ne
vwh (sing.)	becomes	ws ne
yyh[1] (plu.)	becomes	ynhoŋ ne
vwh[2] (plu.)	becomes	wnhoŋ ne[3]

5. Where the object is expressed without <u>ko</u> the verb agrees with
    it in gender and number.

6. Where the object is expressed <u>with ko</u> (or in an equivalent
    form - e.g. <u>mwjhe</u>, <u>wnheŋ</u>, etc.) the form of the verb is always
    that of the masc. sing. in -<u>a</u>.

    There is no quick and easy way of mastering the use of <u>ne</u>.   But
don't let that worry you.   As always, constant practice is the only
way, but you <u>will</u> learn with practice, and the construction will in due
course come quite naturally to you.   Learning by heart the sentences
which you will constantly need in conversation can be very helpful,
for the patterns which they will establish in your head help you towards
correctness in your more conscious and deliberate efforts.   At the same
time there is no escape from the task of remembering and applying all
the information you are given in the statement above.   In translating
into Urdu/Hindi you will need to remember that:

(i)   Most, <u>but not all</u>, transitives take <u>ne</u> in <u>all</u> tenses in
        which the past participle is used.

(ii)   Before <u>ne</u> there is often a change to be made in the form of
        the subject.   (e.g. <u>vwh</u>[2] (plu.) becomes <u>wnhoŋ ne</u>.)

(iii)   Some past participles are irregular.

(iv)   The form of the verb varies according to whether or not the
        object is expressed with -<u>ko</u>.

    With each sentence, therefore, make sure that you have taken into
account <u>all</u> these points (and the detailed elaboration of them in the
statement given above) before you pass on to the next.

---

1. H. ye.
2. H. ve.
3. In H. the <u>ne</u> is commonly not written separately but as part of a
    single word - e.g. <u>wnhoŋ ne</u>.

21.2 Visiting Qudsia

In natural Urdu/Hindi speech or writing you can go on a long
time without finding all of these rules exemplified - a point to which
I'll return shortly.   Meanwhile here is a passage in which you'll
find examples of quite a lot of them.   There'll be quite a lot of
words you don't know, but these are listed and explained after the
passage in the order in which they occur.   (Re-read what I said on
p. 195 above.)

kəl ʃam ko məyŋ əwr swɣraŋ qwdsia ke ghər gəe.   qwdsia ne həmeŋ
khane pər bwlaya tha, əwr sat bəje ke ləg bhəg ane ko kəha tha.   həm sat
bəje se zəra pəhle pəhwŋce.   kar se wtre əwr dərvaze ke pəs jake ghənţi
bəjai.   do mynəţ yntyzar[1] kiya, lekyn koi nəhiŋ aya.   ys liye həm ne
dərvaza khəţkhəţaya.   fəwrən qwdsia aiŋ əwr dərvaza khola.   swɣraŋ ne
kəha, 'həm ne ghənţi bəjai, lekyn koi nəhiŋ aya.   kya ghənţi kam nəhiŋ
kər rəhi?'   qwdsia həŋsiŋ.   kəha, 'nəhiŋ, kam kər rəhi həy, əwr məyŋ ne
ghənţi swni bhi thi, məgər ws vəqt[2] məyŋ khana pəkane meŋ məsruf[3] thi;
fəwrən nəhiŋ a səki'.   həm əndər gəe.   qwdsiya ne həmeŋ byţha diya əwr
xwd həmare sath bəyţh gəiŋ.   ytne meŋ bəcce - wn ke do bəcce həyŋ - pleţeŋ,
chwriyaŋ, kanţe, cəmce - yyh sari cizeŋ lae əwr mez pər rəkh diŋ.   phyr
qwdsia khana laiŋ.   həm khana khate rəhe əwr bateŋ kərte rəhe.   ek məwqe
pər qwdsia ne kəha, 'ap ne yyh xəbər swni hogi ky ynɖiyən armi ne goldən
ţempəl pər qəbza kər liya həy?'   məyŋ ne kəha, 'ji haŋ, yyh xəbər ʃam ke
əxbar meŋ bhi chəpi həy'.   phyr wnhoŋ ne pucha, 'ap ne yyh bhi xəbər swni
həy ky əb bharət jane ke liye viza ki zərurət hogi?'   yyh xəbər həm ne nəhiŋ
swni thi.   khane ke bad qwdsia bərtən kycən meŋ legaiŋ.   həm ne wn ki mədəd
kərni cahi - bərtən dhone cahe - lekyn wnhoŋ ne ws ki yjazət nəhiŋ di.   həmeŋ
byţha diya, əwr xwd bərtən dhoe.   phyr həmeŋ kafi pylai, əwr xwd bhi kafi
pi.   dəs bəje ke qərib həm ne yjazət li, əwr cəle ae.

Notes

kəl	yesterday
ʃam ko	in the evening - note the use of -ko
kəl ʃam ko	'yesterday in the evening' - i.e. last night
bwlana	to invite

---

1.   H. yntəzar.
2.   H. səməy.
3.   H. vyəst.

...ane ko kəha tha   'had said to come...', had told us to come. (This is the standard way of expressing this.)

wtərna   to alight, get out of

   (why wtre? - cf. p.162)

dərvaza   door

jake   having gone, going

ghənʈi   bell

bəjana   'to cause to sound', ring

yntyzar[1] kərna   'to do waiting', to wait

lekyn   but

ys liye   'for this [reason]', so

khəʈkhəʈana   to knock [at]

fəwrən   at once, immediately

kholna   to open (transitive)

kya here simply indicates that the words which follow are a question.

kam kərna   to work

həŋsna   to laugh

məgər   but

ws vəqt[2]   [at] that time

pəkana   to cook

məsruf[3]   engaged, busy

a səkna   to be able to come

   (-səkna means 'to be able'. It never stands on its own, but is always preceded by the root of the verb:

        məyŋ a səkta huŋ
        I (m.) can come

        vwh ja səkti həy
        She (twm status) can go

                    and so on.)

əndər   inside

byʈha dena (treat the two words as one)   'to cause to sit', to ask [someone] to sit down

xwd   self. Here, herself

həmare sath   with us

bəyʈh jana (treat the two words as one)   to sit down

ytne meŋ   in the meanwhile

---

1. H. yntəzar.
2. H. səməy.
3. H. vyəst.

pleṭ	plate
chwri	knife
kanṭa	fork
cəmca	spoon
sara, -i, -e	all
ciz	thing

Note the order = yyh sari cizeŋ.   In Urdu/Hindi the 'all' always comes after the 'this, these, my, your' or whatever.

lana	to bring
mez	table
-pər	-on
rəkh dena (treat the two words as one)	to put
phyr	(1) again, (2) (as here) then
khate rəhe	'remained eating', went on eating
bateŋ kərna	to converse, talk
məwqa	occasion
xəbər	news[-item]
-pər qəbza kər lena (treat the last two words as one)	'to do seizure on-', to seize, capture
əxbar	newspaper
chəpna	to be printed
bharət jane ke liye	for going to India
zərurət	need
bərtən	dishes, plates, etc.
lejana	to take [something or someone somewhere]
-ki mədəd kərna	'to do the help of-', to help
cahna	to wish, want
mədəd kərni cahi	

Note that in such sentences the gender of the object is reflected also in the infinitive and the verb.

dhona	to wash
bərtən dhona	'to wash the dishes', to wash up
yjazət	permission
pylana	'to cause to drink', give [someone something] to drink
yjazət	(1) permission, (2) permission [to depart], leave
yjazət lena	to take leave, say goodbye
cəla ana	to come away

The cəla changes to -i, -e to agree with the subject.

As you see, there is a lot of vocabulary in this passage which is new to you. But as you also see, all of it is within the range of everyday things.

21.3   Five exercises

The main aim of the exercises I'm about to set you is to enable you to get a firmer grasp of the rules I set out at the beginning of this unit. But since the exercises take you back to the passage again and again you'll automatically learn a lot of the vocabulary too.

First I give the passage broken up into separate, numbered sentences. Do these exercises on it.

1.   List the numbers of the sentences – or, better still, <u>write out</u> the sentences, in which the verb is intransitive.

2.   Do the same for sentences in which the verb is transitive, but does not take <u>ne</u>.

3.   Do the same for sentences in which the verb is transitive, and the object is expressed in the direct case (i.e. <u>not</u> the oblique with -<u>ko</u>).

4.   Do the same for sentences in which the object is a sentence or a clause.

5.   Do the same for sentences in which the object is expressed with -<u>ko</u> or a form equivalent to pronoun + <u>ko</u> (mwjhe/mwjh ko, etc.).

On the pages following the passage I have written out the sentences under each of these headings, so that you can check your own work by them.

Visiting Qudsia

1. kəl ʃam ko məyŋ əwr swɣraŋ qwdsia ke ghər gəe.
2. qwdsia ne həmeŋ khane pər bwlaya tha,
3. əwr sat bəje ke ləg bhəg ane ko kəha tha.
4. həm sat bəje se zəra pəhle pəhwŋce.
5. kar se wtre,
6. əwr dərvaze ke pas jake ghənti bəjai.
7. do mynət yntyzar[1] kiya,
8. lekyn koi nəhiŋ aya.
9. ys liye həm ne dərvaza khətkhətaya.
10. fəwrən qwdsia aiŋ
11. əwr dərvaza khola.
12. swɣraŋ ne kəha,
13. 'həm ne ghənti bəjai
14. lekyn koi nəhiŋ aya.
15. kya ghənti kam nəhiŋ kər rəhi?'
16. qwdsia həŋsiŋ.
17. kəha,
18. 'nəhiŋ, kam kər rəhi həy,
19. əwr məyŋ ne ghənti swni bhi thi,
20. məgər ws vəqt[2] məyŋ khana pəkane meŋ məsruf[3] thi;
21. fəwrən nəhiŋ a səki.'
22. həm əndər gəe.
23. qwdsia ne həmeŋ bytha diya
24. əwr xwd həmare sath bəyth gəiŋ.
25. ytne meŋ wn ke bəcce plet, chwriaŋ, kante, cəmce –
    yyh sari cizeŋ lae
26. əwr mez pər rəkh diŋ.
27. phyr qwdsia khana laiŋ.
28. həm khana khate rəhe
29. əwr bateŋ kərte rəhe.
30. ek məwqe pər qwdsia ne kəha,

----

1. H. yntəzar.
2. H. səməy.
3. H. vyəst.

31. 'ap ne yyh xəbər swni hogi

32. ky ynɖiyən armi ne goldən ʈempəl pər qəbza kər liya həy?'

33. məyŋ ne kəha,

34. 'ji haŋ, yyh xəbər ʃam ke əxbar meŋ bhi chəpi həy.'

35. phyr wnhoŋ ne pucha,

36. 'ap ne yyh bhi xəbər swni həy ky

37. əb bharət jane ke liye viza ki zərurət hogi?'

38. yyh xəbər həm ne nəhiŋ swni thi.

39. khane ke bad qwdsia bərtən kycən meŋ legəiŋ.

40. həm ne wn ki mədəd kərni cahi

41. - bərtən dhone cahe -

42. lekyn wnhoŋ ne ws ki y.jazət nəhiŋ di.

43. həmeŋ byʈha diya

44. əwr xwd bərtən dhoe.

45. phyr həmeŋ kafi pylai,

46. əwr xwd bhi kafi pi.

47. dəs bəje ke qərib həm ne yjazət li,

48. əwr cəle ae.

1. <u>Intransitive verbs</u>

1. kəl ʃam ko məyŋ əwr <u>swɣraŋ</u> <u>qwdsia</u> ke ghər gəe.

4. həm sat bəje se zəra pəhle pəhwŋce.

5. (həm) kar se wʈre.

8. koi nəhiŋ aya.

10. fəwrən <u>qwdsia</u> aiŋ.

14. koi nəhiŋ aya.

16. <u>qwdsia</u> həŋsiŋ.

20. ws vəqt[1] məyŋ khana pəkane meŋ məsruf[2] thi.

21. (məyŋ) fəwrən nəhiŋ a səki.

22. həm əndər gəe.

24. (<u>qwdsia</u>/vwh) xwd həmare sath bəyʈh gəiŋ.

_____

1. H. səməy.
2. H. vyəst.

28. həm khana khate rəhe.

29. (həm) bateŋ kərte rəhe.

34. yyh xəbər ʃam ke əxbar meŋ bhi chəpi həy.

37. əb bharət jane ke liye viza ki zərurət hogi?

48. (həm) cəle ae.

2. <u>Transitive verbs without ne</u>

25. ytne meŋ wn ke bəcce pleʈ, chwriəŋ, kanʈe, cəmce - yyh sari
    cizeŋ lae.

27. <u>qwdsia</u> khana laiŋ.

39. khane ke bad <u>qwdsia</u> bərtən kycən meŋ legəiŋ.

3. <u>Transitive verbs with ne</u>

   <u>Objects without ko</u>

6. (həm ne) dərvaze ke pas jake ghənʈi bəjai.

7. (həm ne) do mynəʈ yntyzar[1] kiya.

9. həm ne dərvaza khəʈkhəʈaya.

11. (<u>qwdsia</u>/wnhoŋ ne) dərvaza khola.

13. həm ne ghənʈi bəjai.

19. məyŋ ne ghənʈi swni bhi thi.

26. (bəccoŋ/wnhoŋ ne) (yyh sari cizeŋ) mez pər rəkh diŋ.

31. ap ne yyh xəbər swni hogi

32. ky ynɖiyən armi ne goldən ʈempəl pər qəbza kər liya həy?

36. ap ne yyh bhi xəbər swni həy ky...

38. yyh xəbər həm ne nəhiŋ swni thi.

40. həm ne wn ki mədəd kərni cahi.

41. (həm ne) bərtən dhone cahe.

42. wnhoŋ ne ws ki yjazət nəhiŋ di.

44. (qwdsia/wnhoŋ ne) bərtən dhoe.

45. (qwdsia/wnhoŋ ne) həmeŋ kafi pylai.

46. (qwdsia/wnhoŋ ne) xwd bhi kafi pi.

47. dəs bəje ke qərib həm ne yjazət li.

---

1. H. yntəzar.

4.   <u>With sentence or clause as object</u>

3.   (<u>qwdsia</u> ne) sat bəje ane ko kəha.

12.   <u>swɣraŋ</u> ne kəha...

30.   ek məwqe pər <u>qwdsia</u> ne kəha...

33.   məyŋ ne kəha...

35.   wnhoŋ ne pucha...

5.   <u>Objects expressed with -ko</u> (or equivalent form)

2.   <u>qwdsia</u> ne həmeŋ khane pər bwlaya tha.

23.   <u>qwdsia</u> ne həmeŋ byṭha diya.

43.   (<u>qwdsia/wnhoŋ</u> ne) həmeŋ byṭha diya.

21.4   <u>Retranslation - and what it teaches you</u>

The exercises I've set you so far should have prepared the ground for one a good deal more exacting which I'm going to set you now.

Below you'll find two translations of the passage - the first in natural English and the second in a version as literal as I can make it. Don't look at the second one yet.   Take the first one, and see if you can re-translate it into its original Urdu/Hindi.   You can look at the notes on the passage to remind you of <u>words</u> you don't remember, but don't look at the passage itself.   You'll probably be surprised - but needn't be in the least dismayed! - at how difficult you find this exercise, and at how much of essential detail you don't remember.   If you find the exercise <u>too</u> difficult, take the second translation, the more literal one, and work from that.

Do the best you can, and don't be upset if that best doesn't come up to your expectations.   Where there are bits you can't manage, leave them out.   When you've done what you can, compare it with the original Urdu/Hindi passage.

As before when you did a similar exercise, you needn't assume that where your version differs from the original passage it will necessarily be wrong, but you <u>know</u> that the original passage is O.K., so make that your model for further work.

After you've done this exercise I shall say something about what it is intended to teach you.

Natural translation

Last night Sughran and I went to Qudsia's house.   Qudsia
had invited us to a meal, and had told us to come about seven.   We
got there a little before seven, got out of the car, and went to the
door and rang the bell.   We waited a couple of minutes, but no one
came.   So we knocked at the door.   At once Qudsia came and opened
the door.   Sughran said, 'We rang the bell, but nobody came.   Isn't
the bell working?'   Qudsia laughed.   She said, 'No, it's working,
and I heard it, but I was busy with the cooking and couldn't come at
once.'   We went in.   Qudsia asked us to sit down, and sat down with
us.   Meanwhile the children - she has two children - brought
plates, knives, forks, spoons - all those things, and put them on the
table.   Then Qudsia brought the food.   We ate and talked at the same
time.   At one point Qudsia said, 'You'll have heard the news that the
Indian army has seized the Golden Temple?'   I said, 'Yes, the news is
in the evening paper too.'   Then she asked, 'And have you also heard
the news that now you'll need a visa to go to India?'   We hadn't heard
that.   After the meal Qudsia took the dishes into the kitchen.   We
wanted to help her - wanted to do the washing up - but she wouldn't let
us.   She told us to sit down, and washed up herself.   Then she gave us
coffee, and had coffee with us.   About 10 o'clock we said goodbye and
left.

Literal translation

Yesterday in the evening I and Sughran went to Qudsia's house.
Qudsia had invited us to a meal and had said to come about seven o'clock.
We arrived a little before seven o'clock.   ⌊We⌋ got down from the car
and, going to ('near') the door, rang the bell.   Two minutes ⌊we⌋
waited, but no-one came.   So we knocked ⌊at⌋ the door.   At once Qudsia
came and opened the door.   Sughran said, 'We rang the bell, but no-one
came.   Is the bell not working?'   Qudsia laughed.   [She] said, 'No,
[it]'s working, and I heard the bell too, but [at] that time I was busy
in cooking the food; [I] couldn't come at once.   We went inside.
Qudsia seated us and herself sat down with us.   In the meanwhile the

children - she has two children - brought plates, knives, forks,
spoons - all these things and put them on the table.   Then Qudsia
brought the food.   We went on eating food and went on talking.   On
one occasion Qudsia said, 'You'll have heard this news-item that the
Indian army has seized ('made grip on') the Golden Temple?'   I said,
'Yes, this news-item has been printed in the evening newspaper too.'
Then she said, 'Have you heard this news-item too that now for going
to India there will be need of a visa?'   This news-item we had not
heard.   After the meal Qudsia took-away the dishes in[to] the kitchen.
We wanted to help her ['do her help'], but she did not give permission
for ['of'] that.   She seated us, and herself washed the dishes.   Then
she caused us to drink coffee and herself also drank coffee.   About
10 o'clock we took leave and came away.

What an exercise like this ought to teach you

When you first encounter a piece of Urdu/Hindi, you naturally
(and quite properly) aim first at understanding it.   But when you've
done that, you need to return to it again and again until you feel
that you've understood everything in it, and registered what every
word and phrase in it does.   Re-translation is the surest test you
can give yourself, and the surest way of learning what else you need
to register and assimilate over and above what you have already done.
Even when you're provided with an English version and a list of
Urdu/Hindi words you'll be surprised at how much of the information
you needed you've failed to register.   In doing the exercise you've
just done I expect some of you found that you hadn't registered the
genders of words.   (I deliberately didn't give the genders.   You
ought to know by now how you can list words in a way that shows you
their genders.)   Or perhaps you hadn't remembered that 'to help her'
in Urdu/Hindi is 'to do her help'.   The experience ought to help you
to enhance your ability to register such things as you read.

If you are learning in class, there are other ways of helping you
to learn these things.   And even if you aren't, there are useful
exercises you can design for yourselves.   For example, you can take
the passage down at the 'dictation' of the cassette, or, you can write
out the passage leaving gaps here and there with a clue in English in
their place, and then see if, without looking at the original, you can
fill in the gaps correctly.   Like this:

həm qwdsia [to the house of] gəe

bəcce yyh sari [things][brought] əwr mez pər [put]

I don't suggest you do all these exercises in quick succession! You can return to the passage at intervals and do a different exercise on it each time.

When you're fairly thoroughly familiar with the passage it's not difficult - (and it's a very good idea) - to learn it by heart. You'll find that by doing so you learn a great deal more than you realise you're learning, and that it stands you in very good stead as you go further.

21.5 Exercise by drilling

I think that at this stage it is sensible to practise you intensively in the full range of structures associated with ne. I said earlier that in natural Urdu/Hindi speech or writing you can go a long time without finding all of the rules exemplified. And yet they are so common, and so fundamental to correct usage that you need to acquire and practise them to the point where they come quickly and naturally to you.

If you're studying in a class there are various ways in which your teachers can practise you, but you can also practise on your own. Here are two pages of bits of sentences which include all the possible variations - the first in Urdu/Hindi, and the second in English. Take the Urdu/Hindi page first. Put together a sentence, and translate it into English. Then check with the other page to make sure you've got it right. The numbering in the two numbered columns matches the Urdu/Hindi and the English versions.

Then take your English version of the sentence and put it back into Urdu-Hindi, checking with the Urdu/Hindi page.

You may find it useful to re-read the full rules set out on pages 198-9 before you start this exercise, and to refer back to them whenever you feel the need.

dekha/dekha həy/dekha tha/dekha hoga
dekhi/dekhi həy/dekhi thi/dekhi hogi
dekhe/dekhe həyŋ/dekhe the/dekhe hoŋge
dekhiŋ/dekhi həyŋ/dekhi thiŋ/dekhi hoŋgi

1.	məyŋ ne	1.	yyh drama	
2.	twm ne	2.	yyh¹ drame	
3.	ap ne	3.	yyh təsvir	
5,9.	ys ne	4.	yyh¹ təsvireŋ	
7,11.	ws ne	5.	yyh admi	
4,8,13.	ynhoŋ ne	6.	yyh¹ admi	
6,10,14.	wnhoŋ ne	7.	yyh ləṛki	
12.	həm ne	8.	yyh¹ ləṛkiyaŋ	
15.	mere beṭe ne	9.	mwjh ko, mwjhe	
16.	mere bhai ne	10.	twm ko, twmheŋ	
17.	meri beṭi ne	11.	ap ko	
18.	meri bəhyn ne	13,17.	ys ko, yse	
19.	mere beṭoŋ ne	14,15,19.	ws ko, wse	
20.	mere bhaiyoŋ ne	12,16,18,21.	yn ko, ynheŋ	
21.	meri beṭiyoŋ ne	22.	wn ko, wnheŋ	
22.	meri bəhynoŋ ne	20.	həm ko, həmeŋ	
		23.	choṭe ləṛke ko	
		24.	choṭi ləṛki ko	
		25.	choṭe ləṛkoŋ ko	
		26.	choṭi ləṛkiyoŋ ko	
		27.	choṭe bhai ko	
		28.	choṭi bəhyn ko	
		29.	choṭe bhaiyoŋ ko	
		30.	choṭi bəhynoŋ ko	

1. H. ye.

saw/have seen/had seen/will have seen

1. I
2. you (junior)
3. you
4. he (equal and present)
5. he (junior and present)
6. he (equal and not present)
7. he (junior and not present)
8. she (equal and present)
9. she (junior and present)
10. she (equal and not present)
11. she (junior and not present)
12. we
13. they (present)
14. they (not present)
15. my son
16. my brother
17. my daughter
18. my sister
19. my sons
20. my brothers
21. my daughters
22. my sisters

---

*1. this play (drama m.)
2. these plays
3. this picture (tasvir, f.)
4. these pictures
5. this man (admi)
6. these men
7. this girl
8. these girls
**9. me
10. you (twm)
11. you (ap)
12. him (equal and present)
13. him (junior and present)
14. him (equal and not present)
15. him (junior and not present)
16. her (equal and present)
17. her (junior and present)
18. her (equal and not present)
19. her (junior and not present)
20. us
21. them (present)
22. them (not present)
23. the younger boy
24. the younger girl
25. the younger boys
26. the younger girls
27. the younger brother
28. the younger sister
29. the younger brothers
30. the younger sisters

---

* For numbers 1-8 use the direct form
** For numbers 9-30 use -ko (or equivalent form)

Where do you go from here?

When you've mastered all that you've learned so far you'll have grasped all the most essential features of the language, and will be thinking of what you are to do next.

Well, first, don't think you've finished with this book. Unless you keep re-acquainting yourself with everything in it you'll find that there are things you'll forget. So read, and re-read, and re-read it, noting at each re-reading everything that hasn't really stuck, and not ceasing to re-read it from time to time until you find that it's all there - in your head, to come readily to your tongue when you speak. As I have told you from the start, you will help yourself a lot if you learn by heart whole sentences from these units. Above all, maintain all the time your ability to speak correctly and fluently. I told you at the beginning (How to use this book) ways of doing this. (Read it again and refresh your memory!) If you find it helpful to come to classes the best pattern is to plan to attend a series of short intensive courses at intervals of say, not more than six months, and to make sure that you work regularly in between them. Attending intensive courses, and working in pairs, or threes, or fours between them, is a far more effective way to learn than a simple attendance at a 2 hours a week course - though that too can, of course, be useful.

Let me repeat what I also told you at the start - that you should use such Urdu/Hindi as you have from the very beginning, not only in class class, but, so to speak, in real life outside the class. Most Urdu/Hindi speakers are very happy to help you, and the more you use your Urdu/Hindi the more rapidly you will extend the range of the things you can say in it. Go on doing this. A few simple sentences will help you over difficulties. You already know how to ask someone to repeat what s/he's said. If you want her/him to speak more slowly you can say

> zəra ah**ysta** boliye
> slowly

Where you hear a word you don't understand, try to isolate it and ask what it means. For example, if someone says

> vwh bəhwt pəre∫an həy

and you don't know what pəre∫an means, say

> 'pəre∫an' ke mani kya həyŋ?[1]

What's the meaning of 'pəre∫an'? i.e. What does 'pəre∫an' mean? (It means, 'worried, anxious, upset'.)

(Notice the ke mani kya həyŋ[1] - i.e. that the Urdu word is plural, although the English word 'meaning' is singular.)

---

1. H. ka ərth kya həy.

And if you don't know the Urdu/Hindi for something - e.g. 'shoe' - ask

> 'shoe' ko wrdu[1] meŋ kya kəhte həyŋ?
> What do they call 'shoe' in Urdu?[2]
> i.e. What's shoe in Urdu?[2]
>   What's the Urdu[2] for shoe?

(Notice that kəhna in this sentence means not 'to say', but 'to call'.)

Some people will reply when you ask them their name

> mwjhe ...... kəhte həyŋ
> 'They call me .....', i.e. 'My name is .....')

Or, if you want to know how to say something in Urdu/Hindi, say the English sentence and ask

> ap yse wrdu[1] meŋ kəyse kəheŋge?
> How would (literally, 'will') you (i.e. 'one')
> say this in Urdu?[2]

You can learn a lot by operating with these simple phrases.

I've already said that your main need from now on will be to extend the range of your vocabulary. Part III, with its accompanying reference book Part II, will help you to do this. Don't regard the passages in Part III as material simply to be read and understood. Think all the time of how you will use what you read in speaking to people. It's not difficult to take the vocabulary and structures used in passages about other people, and work out how to adapt them to serve your needs and say the things you want to say. If you do that you're bound almost automatically to make progress all the time. Of course, there's no end to this process. You'll go on learning more and more for as long as you use the language. But that's true of any language, including your own.

When I wrote Parts II and III I thought of them as materials from which a student could make rapid progress even if she were working entirely on her own, and provided you use them in the way I've just described, I'm sure that you can do that. But a good many students like to continue to work with teachers, and to be set particular tasks based upon the Part III materials. To help them, Ian Russell, Marion Molteno and others have prepared supplementary materials to Part III, and I hope that these will shortly be published.

Part IV teaches you to write the Urdu script, and you will do yourselves a lot of good in the eyes of Urdu speakers if you learn it. (Literacy in the language is generally regarded by them as, to say the least, not less important than oral command.) At the time of writing, all those I know who began their learning of Urdu with Part I and can now read and write the Urdu script well, learnt it entirely on their own, using Part IV, and it did not take them very long to do so. So I hope you will feel encouraged to follow their example!

---

1. hyndi

2. Hindi

Those of you who are learning Hindi can learn the Hindi (Devanagari) script relatively easily. It is a very systematic script, and, generally speaking, follows the one sound, one symbol principle. Most Hindi language courses set it out at the very beginning, and you could learn it from any such course.

Appendices

1. The script used in this course

2. Greetings

3. Numbers 1-31, and dates

Appendix 1

The script used in this course

I explained in unit 1 the reason why I use this script (invented not by me but by Professor J.R.Firth) and why, if you're wise, you'll take care to learn it.   If you do, you'll always be able to note accurately any new word you hear, and will always be able to read it back accurately when you look at it again, even if in the meantime you've forgotten what it means.   And if you don't, you <u>won't</u> be able to do that.   Once you've made up your mind that you <u>need</u> to learn it, the script is not in the least difficult to learn.

Wherever possible it uses the letters of the English alphabet to represent sounds which, near enough, match those of English.   Here are these letters, in English alphabetical order.   (Note the ones that are missing!   These are going to be used in another way.)

b   f   g   h   j   k   l   m   n   p   r   s   z

What about the ones that are missing from this list?

First, you'll notice that all the vowels are missing.   I'll say something about this in a moment.

Secondly, there are letters missing which even English doesn't in fact need, because, for example, 'c' standing on its own always represents the same sound as either 'k' or 's', and 'x' represents a sound that can also perfectly well be represented by 'ks'.   So we take these letters out and use them for other sounds.

Thirdly, you'll notice that there's no 'd' and no 't' in the list. That's because there are <u>two</u> 'd'-like, and <u>two</u> 't'-like, sounds in Urdu/ Hindi, and neither of the pair is the same as the English 'd' and 't' sounds.   We use 'd' and 't' to represent one of the pair and a modified version for the other one of the pair.

So:

The vowels

Experts in phonetics say that speakers of southern English use twenty-one different vowels - and have to make do with five letters

a   e   i   o   u

(plus some combinations of these and other letters) to represent them.

Not surprisingly, it doesn't make a very good job of it.   Take 'a' for example.   It stands for a different sound in each of the following words about, alien, bat, bark

and the list could be extended.

In the script we use for this course each vowel-letter (or pair of letters) stands for one sound and one sound only. These were set out and explained in unit 1, where you will find more detail than I give here. Here they are, with Urdu words that exemplify them.

ə	kəhiye
a	ap ka nam
y	phyr
	(y is also used to represent the consonant y)
i	bəʃir
w	swniye
u	puchiye
e	mera, kəhiye
əy	həy
o	som
əw	əwr, əwrət

Other 'missing' letters

'c' is used to represent the sound similar to that which English usually represents as 'ch'. (For what 'ch' means in our script, see below.) Those of you who know some Italian will be familiar with its use for this sound.

Examples: cae, car, cəca

'd'	- see below
'q'	- as in qərib, təqribən (See page 44.)
'v'	- as in vəhaŋ - it's about half-way between an English 'v' and an English 'w'. (See p.23)
'x'	- as in bavərcixana (See page 134.)

d and ḍ; t and ṭ - and ṛ

We use 'd' and 't' to represent the dental sounds, and
'ḍ' and 'ṭ' to represent the retroflex sounds.

These were described in unit 1 (p.13).

There is also a retroflex 'ṛ' - as in pəṛhna.

Aspiration

In Hindi and Urdu very many consonants have an aspirated and an unaspirated version, and it's important that you should distinguish them clearly in pronunciation.   There are some, but only some, that don't come easily to English speakers; but these are easily acquired if you make the minimal effort you need.   In this script we represent aspiration by adding an 'h' after the letter that stands for the unaspirated sound.

'kh', 'bh', etc. of course really represent a single sound.   (In the Devanagari (Hindi) script, which is a much more scientific one than either English or Urdu, aspirated and unaspirated consonants each have a single letter to represent them.)   Make sure that you always pronounce them as single sounds.

Note that 'ch', 'ph', 'th' never represent the sounds they do in English.

ŋ, ʃ and ɣ

ŋ doesn't represent a separate sound, but simply indicates that the vowel which comes before it is nasalised.

ʃ stands for the sound usually represented in English by 'sh'.

ɣ - the sound exemplified in ɣwsəlxana.

You have live speakers and/or cassettes to help you acquire a good pronunciation, and I've generally not attempted to use English words to exemplify Urdu sounds.   In my experience most people acquire the sounds perfectly well by repeated imitation, and it's only rarely helpful to give any other guidance.   Where it is helpful, I've offered it, but not elsewhere.   You'll often acquire a correct pronunciation without even realising that you're using an un-English sound.   For example, the 'l' of kəl is not the same sound as the 'l' in English 'milk'.   (Notice how South Asians who use their own pronunciation patterns for English pronounce this word, and you'll see the difference at once.)   But though it is quite correct to say that the 'l' of kəl is pronounced with the tongue flat and relaxed, if you're pronouncing it that way without being told, then why tell you?

Speech habits die hard, so don't assume that because in speaking Hindi/Urdu you can make the difference between p and ph quite clearly heard, you always will.   You'll always need to take care with your pronunciation; but you shouldn't find that too much of a burden.

Appendix 2

Greetings

There are no generally current greeings in Hindi/Urdu that
are free of religious associations.   Programmes on TV and radio for
Asian audiences use hello (in roman script <u>helo</u>) and goodbye (<u>gwd</u> <u>bai</u>).

Otherwise the following are used:

<u>Hindus</u>:   nəməste, or nəməskar (homage).
                     Repeated in reply.

<u>Muslims</u>:   əssəlam ələykwm (peace be upon you).

and in reply: <u>valəykwm</u> <u>əssəlam</u> (and upon you be peace).

on leaving: <u>xwda</u> <u>hafyz</u> (God protector).   Repeated
                     in reply.

<u>Sikhs</u>:   <u>sət</u> <u>sri</u> <u>əkal</u> ('truth is immortal').
                     Repeated in reply.

You will find a fuller account of these and other courtesies in
Part II.

Appendix 3

Numbers, dates, months

To tell the time exactly, and to state the date, you need to know the numbers up to 31.   Here they are:

1.	ek	17.	satra
2.	do	*18.	atthara
3.	tin	*19.	wnnis
4.	car	20.	bis
5.	panc	*21.	ykkis
6.	chay	22.	bais
7.	sat	23.	teis
8.	ath	24.	cawbis
9.	naw	*25.	paccis
10.	das	*26.	chabbis
11.	gyara	*27.	sattais
12.	bara	*28.	atthais
13.	tera	*29.	wnattis (or, wntis)
14.	cawda	30.	tis
15.	pandra	*31.	ykattis (or yktis)
16.	sola		

Dates

The word for 'date' is 'tarix'.

<u>aj kya tarix hay?</u>

means   Today what date is?
i.e. What is the date today?

You would reply:

<u>aj mangal, pandra August (agast)[1] hay.</u>
'Today is Tuesday fifteen August'
i.e. Today is Tuesday, the fifteenth of August.

---

1. See below.

---

*   Note the double consonants.

Note that you would say

aj pəhli August (əgəst)[1] həy
Today is the first [of] August

(pəhl<u>i</u> to agree with <u>tarix</u> understood.)

and could say <u>dusri</u>, <u>tisri</u>, though <u>do</u>, <u>tin</u> are at least as common.

             2nd   3rd   2   3

From the 4th onwards, <u>car</u>, <u>pəɲc</u>, <u>chəy</u> etc. are much more common than

                               4   5

the words meaning 'fourth, fifth, sixth', and so on.

Strictly speaking, the names of the months are:

> jənvəri
>
> fərvəri
>
> marc
>
> əprəyl
>
> məi
>
> jun
>
> julai   (Note that in Urdu <u>all three</u> of the vowels are
>
              long.   In Hindi j<u>w</u>lai is usual.)
>
əgəst
>
> sytəmbər
>
> əktubər
>
> nəvəmbər
>
> dysəmbər

But people settled here will often use the English pronunciation (more or less) and you won't be misunderstood if you do too.

You'll find a full account of the numbers, and their use, and the best way to learn them, in Part II.

---

1. See below.

Index of Urdu/Hindi words

(Words which are only Urdu are in brackets.)

The numbers refer to units.   I didn't think it necessary to index units after the first part of 18.   Generally I've given only the first unit in which the word occurs.   I've not indicated words like nam; you're not likely to forget these.

The order in which I give the words will soon become clear to you. The vowels come first, and the consonants in English alphabetical order, except that I have put all words beginning with 'bh' after the 'b' section, and so on with 'ch', 'dh', etc.   'ɣ' comes immediately after 'gh'.

əwrət	14	bhər	
əwrəteŋ	2	dyn bhər	9
		bhai	7
bəcce	6	bharət	4
bəcca	6	bhi	2
bəcci	6		
bəhyn,		cəca	15
bəhyneŋ	7	(cəca-zad)	15
bəhwt	1	cae	9
bəhu	9	car	4
...bəje		caroŋ, etc.	6
= [at]... o'clock			
	9	chwʈʈi	16
bəjkər	17	chəy	4
bəngladeʃ	4	choʈa	4
bəjna	17	choʈa sa	4
...bəjne meŋ	17	choʈi	7
bənd	13		
bəngali	14	dəfa	10, 15
bərəs	17	do dəfa	10
bəṛa	4	dəftər	9
bəṛi	7	dəftər pəhwŋcna	
bəṛi bəṛi	4		9
bətaiye	1	dəraz	13
bais	11	dərvaza	13
baɣica	13	dəs	9
bara	9	dyn	10, 17
bathrum	13	dar wl hwkumət	4
(bavərcixana)	13	diya, di, die, diŋ	
(bivi)	5		18
bis	10	dudh	18
(berozgar)	2	dukan	13
beʈa, beʈe	6	dur	4
beʈi, beʈiyaŋ	6	dusra	13
bəyʈhiye	8	dusri dəfa	10
bolna	14	dekh bhal	9
		dekhiye	6

Index of Hindi words

Index of grammar etc.

I give here only the key references. For further detail you can look at the Contents.